Hidden Victims
Hidden Healers

Hidden Victims Hidden Healers

An Eight-Stage Healing Process
for Family and Friends
of the Mentally Ill

JULIE TALLARD JOHNSON

Published by PEMA Publications Inc.,
P.O. Box 24598, Edina, MN 55424

First Edition Published by Doubleday, a division of Bantam Doubleday Dell

Library of Congress Cataloging-in-Publication Data

Johnson, Julie Tallard.
Hidden Victims/Hidden Healers: an eight-stage healing process for families and
friends of the mentally ill /Julie Tallard Johnson.—1st ed., 1988, Doubleday.
p.cm.
Bibliography: p.
1. Mentally ill—Family relationships. 2. Adjustment (Psychology)
1. Title.
RC455.4.F3J63 1994 94-065648
155.9'16—dc19 CIP

ISBN: 0-9640430-0-9
Copyright 1994, 1988 by Julie Johnson
All rights reserved.
Printed in the United States of America
September 1988
First Edition
March 1994
Second Edition

Grateful acknowledgment is made for permission to reprint the following: Excerpt
from Living in the Light by Shakti Gawain with Laurel King. Copyright © 1986 by
Shakti Gawain. Reprinted by permission of New World Library, San Rafael,
California.
Excerpt from The Courage to Create by Rollo May. Copyright © 1975 by Rollo May.
Used by permission of W. W. Norton & Company, Inc.
Excerpt from Stage Two Recovery by Earnie Larsen. Copyright © 1987 by Earnie
Larsen. Reprinted by permission of Harper & Row.
"I Live My Life in Growing Orbits" by Rainer Maria Rilke, and one additional excerpt
from the book The Selected Poems of Rainer Maria Rilke, translated by Robert
Bly. Copyright © 1981 by Robert Bly. Reprinted by permission of Harper & Row.
Excerpt Iron "The Gift Outright" from The Poetry of Robert Frost, edited by Edward
Connery Lathem. Copyright © 1942 Holt, Rinehart, and Winston, Inc. Reprinted
with permission of Henry Holt and Company, Inc.
Excerpt from The Wisdom of No Escape, by Pema Chödrön, 1991, Shambhala
Publications.

For my parents,
my brothers and sisters,
and my friend Mary

with love

Acknowledgments

This book was written using the experiences, knowledge, and help of many special people. For all their wisdom and support I am forever grateful.

I want to first acknowledge the great many people who cannot be thanked by name, the family members and clients who were gracious enough to share their experiences. It is to them I am most indebted and without them, this book and the Eight Stage Healing Process would not have been possible. Thank you.

Thank you, Rachel Klayman, for your exceptional editorial talents, commitment to excellence, and encouragement, all of which are reflected on each page of this book.

Thank you, Jill Breckenridge, for first helping me "confront the empty page," and for your trained eye and heart as a writing consultant.

Thank you Kristine Merrill, mostly for your friendship but also for your dedication to the Eight Stage Healing Process.

Thank you, Jere Truer, for being such a decent human being and for helping me take more risks in my own writing.

Thank you Virginia E. Jacobson, for keeping the spirit of this program alive.

Thank you Tamara Truer for being here now.

Finally, I am most thankful to the Greater Power in the Universe that makes it possible for this book and its message to reach you.

Contents

1 Disrupted Lives   1

2 You Can Heal Anything You Can Name   28

3 The Caretakers   48

4 The Escape Artists   66

5 A Delicate Balance   83

6 Making Decisions You Can Live With   107

7 Breaking the Silence   141

8 The Eight Stages   156

9 Reaching Out For Help   186

Eight Stage Resources   201

AUTHOR'S NOTE

In an effort to safeguard the privacy of my clients, I have made multiple alterations of detail in every one of the many personal accounts and case histories given in this book. Although each story is based upon real events, I have in every case changed names, disguised identifying characteristics, and, in some cases, created composite characters to avoid identification.

I live my life in growing orbits
which move out over the things of the world.
Perhaps I can never achieve the last,
but that will be my attempt.

I am circling around God, around the ancient tower,
and I have been circling for a thousand years,
and I still don't know if I am a falcon, or a storm,
or a great song.

—RAINER MARIA RILKE

Hidden Victims
Hidden Healers

1

Disrupted Lives

The needle that pierces may carry a thread that binds us to heaven.

— JAMES HASTINGS

Karen remembers how Doug woke her one evening last month telling her he was Jesus Christ. And wasn't it time she was baptized? That was before he was convinced he was Lee Harvey Oswald because he owned a Lee jean jacket and had the middle name of Lee. A rifle sat in his closet in case the police found him. Most of the time he hid in Karen's room. But he gave the gun up after his summit meetings with the President—about which he so often spoke. Today Karen looks with sadness at Doug's matted black hair and tired eyes. Now he hears voices from the portraits warning him that the family is poisoning him.

Karen's brother has schizophrenia. And as her story illustrates, the mental illness affects her too. Like alcoholism, mental illness often disables the entire family. Indeed, anyone interacting with a person who behaves like Doug is changed. No one can live with such behaviors as paranoia, intense emotional swings, or depression and not be affected.

In the United States alone, one in four families has a mentally ill loved one. One of every one hundred Americans is believed to be afflicted with schizophrenia. Psychiatric disorders are the number one reason for hospital admissions in this country and are more common than cancer, diabetes, heart dis-ease, and arthritis combined. But the effects of mental illness are not just limited to those with the disorders. Mental illness is a dis-ease which brings millions of families to crisis.

The body and mind naturally goes towards a state of health and balance—that is, *being at ease*. When we are out of balance, out of ease, we are *dis-eased* in some way. When we are dis-eased we are somehow blocked from our health. So, our goal and responsibility is to clear the blocks to our health and well-being. Mental illness is a dis-ease which takes individuals and families out of balance and harmony. Mental illness, therefore, is a family dis-ease.

The effects on the family are universal, though the characteristics of the dis-ease may vary from severe depression to paranoia. Mental illness, as referred to here, includes schizophrenia, bipolar disorder, long term depression, borderline personality disorder, other character disorders, and extreme phobias. To bridge the differences between these illnesses, a simple definition of mental illness will be applied to them all: Mental illness is a dis-ease which causes a prolonged disruption in an individual's ability to function psychologically, socially, emotionally, economically, and spiritually.

All mental/emotional illnesses, especially when untreated, interfere with one's relationships, interpersonal and communication skills, and ability to handle stress, as well as one's thought and emotional patterns. When someone is paranoid, he may withdraw. When someone hears voices, he may assume that it is God talking to him and take the messages literally.

When someone is depressed, he may not get out of bed. When such symptoms as paranoid delusions, social phobia, hallucinations, or depression exist for an extended period of time, a person's life can become overwhelmed by these symptoms.

Often, these symptoms are not recognized as a mental illness and the disabling effects on the individual and family worsen because the illness goes undiagnosed. Often, the ill person will continue to deny the seriousness of the problem in spite of others telling him he needs help, or he may not receive help because disabling symptoms, such as paranoia or depression, prevent him from seeking help on his own.

Families of the mentally ill are often reluctant to view mental illness as a dis-ease that affects every family member. Family members avoid taking a closer look at how the mental illness affects them because such a perspective may lead them to blame themselves. They may also feel inhibited by the social stigma surrounding mental illness. Stigma is often expressed by biases and misconceptions about the family of the mentally ill individual: "If you have a crazy father, you must be sick too"; "Schizophrenia is caused by unstable and uncaring mothers"; "There must be something very wrong with your family." These attitudes make the well family members reluctant to seek help for themselves, since doing so feels like an admission that something is wrong with them.

However, as mental illness is increasingly understood as a dis-ease that affects the family as a whole, there will be less focus on blame and more on solutions. Family members will be looked upon less as a cause of mental illness and more as the "hidden victims and hidden healers." Such understanding de-mystifies mental illness, enabling families to talk about the dis-ease.

This is not to say that the family environment does not in any way contribute to an individual's mental or emotional health. Certainly environmental factors, which include emotional, psychological and physical abuse can and do contribute to the causes of mental illness. Just as a healthy environment free of pollution adds to the health of those living in the area; a family free of abuse and neglect will contribute to the health of each member. Getting caught up in blame and shame is not a solution here, as the following tale illustrates.

Three travelers were walking down a path with important destinations on their mind. As they walked, they came upon a beautiful crystal and gold vase that had broken. Next to the broken vase was a large rock. The first traveler became angry and frustrated over seeing such a beautiful vase all broken. She asked, "How did this happen? *Who* did this? Did the vase hit the rock or did the rock smash the vase?" This question caused her such confusion she sat down in anguish trying to figure it out. The second traveler felt anger and grief, *"Why?,"* he asked, "Why did this happen? It was once such a beautiful vase, why would God let such a thing occur?" And this question caused the traveler to sink into a deep state of hopelessness and helplessness and he sat unable to move. The third traveler, agreed that it was a sad thing that such a beautiful vase would have such a tragedy. She did not ask who or why but instead said, "I am not sure why or how this happened; the vase is broken either way." She bent over and gently picked up the broken pieces of the vase and went on her way.

The question is not why or how but *what?* What is happening and what is the next action that can be taken. This chapter, as well as the entire book focuses on the *what—* what happens to the relationships and the lives of those who care about someone with mental or emotional illness. The idea is to become the traveler who picks up the broken pieces and gets on with our journey. Who do we help by getting stuck in the why's and how's? We help no one.

Like alcoholism, mental illness interferes with healthy family relationships. Family members respond to mental illness much as they would to alcoholism. Common characteristics of those with mental illness and alcoholism include unpredictable behavior, withdrawal, suspicion of others, manipulative behaviors, and disordered thoughts. Common family responses to these characteristics include frustration, confusion, anger, secrecy, hopelessness, covering up for the ill person's disruptive or illegal behavior, and denial of the dis-ease and its effects. Neither families of the alcoholic nor the mentally ill should wait until the person with the dis-ease begins to recover before seeking help for themselves. The dis-eased person too often denies he has a problem or refuses to be active in any kind of treatment program, if he does recognize a problem. Families' and friends' lives would be progressively disrupted by the dis-ease of the ill person if they were to wait for him to accept the needed help. Thus, families must learn ways to live effectively with mental illness, and not allow the disease to permeate and disrupt every aspect of family life.

This chapter describes five phases that characterize family relationships during the course of a mental illness. The first two phases, Early Warnings and Keeping the Peace, deal with the reactions of family members as a loved one's behavior becomes increasingly disturbed. In the third phase, Rude Awakening, the family seeks help and may receive the diagnosis of mental illness. During this phase families experience a series of crises which seriously interfere with family stability. Then, after living in crisis, families begin to adjust in the Just Coping phase. Here family members adopt coping skills which allow them to survive their chaotic family life. Unfortunately, most families never move beyond this phase.

Although families who have a mentally ill loved one vary in social, economic, and religious backgrounds, they have one thing in common: every family member is damaged by the family's inability to deal effectively with the mental illness. This book is intended to help families move beyond Just Coping into the fifth phase, A Delicate Balance, which consists of creating alternative ways to live with the disabling effects of mental illness and the disruption it brings to the family. Since mental illness affects everyone in the family—

siblings, children, parents, and spouses—answers must be found for everyone, not only for the one who is mentally ill. In this final phase family members find hope and solutions to the many challenges they each face.

PHASE ONE: EARLY WARNINGS

Unlike alcoholism or even mental retardation, mental illness is not accompanied by commonly known warning signs. When mental illness first manifests itself, families are usually unaware of the magnitude of the dis-ease and often attribute the change in behavior to other causes, reassuring themselves that, "She's a troubled adolescent," "She's moody," or "He's just in a phase."

Most people respond to such crises as dis-ease, death, or natural disasters with the hope and expectation that everything will soon return to normal. This is natural to expect things will return to normal. Because of this expectation, families of the mentally ill often ignore signs of trouble. They meet the initial exposure to mental illness without any understanding of what they are up against. They observe the odd behavior of a loved one with the expectation that he will get through it.

Something peculiar is happening to Craig's younger sister, Jamie. She acts more agitated than usual and is less interested in making the homemade candles that used to occupy much of her free time. Craig notices an uneasiness about the way Jamie moves around the house, darting in and out of rooms as if she were searching for something. Just yesterday she asked Craig if "God punished evil people by entering their brains and telling them to die." Late last night she was singing to herself, but maybe it was crying he heard. As he watched her dart into another room he wondered if this was normal behavior for a fifteen-year-old girl.

Kimberly was afraid of her father these days. He always acted in ways that scared and embarrassed her but now he withdrew into his "den" and didn't talk to anyone. He didn't care if she came or went. He didn't know that just last week she didn't get home until two in the morning. She likes the freedom but she's worried about him. Kimberly's mother died five years ago, leaving Kimberly at the age of seventeen, alone with her father.

Early warning signs of mental illness may include withdrawal from social interaction, deviation from previous beliefs and routines, suspicion of others, agitated behavior, or hypersensitivity in family disputes. When several of these symptoms are present, it is a warning that a person may be afflicted with mental illness. Rare is the family that recognizes such early warning signs.

Because families expect and hope that the loved one's behavior will return to normal spontaneously, family members are likely to feel impatient and bewildered when such improvement does not happen. They don't know how to help or react to the person who shows these signs of change. Confused, they keep quiet, partly because they do not want to add to each other's burdens and also because it is not clear to them what they need to talk about.

During this phase of Early Warnings, parents and spouses of the mentally ill may believe they should be able to control all the family's problems. Unable to do so, they feel guilty and cannot openly discuss their concerns with the rest of the family. At this time, the siblings and children of the mentally ill usually do not question their parents' coping strategies. Family members begin to build a protective wall of silence around their confusion and the expectations they hold for one another's behavior.

Emily tells what is was like for her family when she was growing up: "My mother was always different from other mothers," explains Emily. "One day she would be playful, like one of us kids, and the next she wouldn't come out of her room. I often wondered if this was how all mothers acted. Somehow I knew it wasn't. I stopped inviting friends over because I could never be sure how she would behave. My father never sat us down and talked with us. I guess he didn't know what to tell us."

Family members not only attempt to protect one another by their silence, they also attempt to protect themselves from acknowledging a greater fear—that the problems may not just go away.

Samantha remembers the time her brother first showed signs of trouble: "I felt something was wrong, but nobody was talking about it. I didn't know what to say to my parents. I wish they'd talked about John and why he was behaving so strangely. I was so alone. I felt like the most awful thing was happening to my brother and my family. But I was never quite sure what it was. I can remember being so frightened. I'd stay up nights praying to God to help my brother. I wonder now if my parents were frightened too. I don't know why we didn't share our concerns. I think if we had just talked about how scared we were, we would have felt better. But we didn't discuss it—then or now."

Many families remain trapped in this isolation and silence for years, hiding their fears, secretly hoping and praying for solutions. Many expect the trouble will end if they just wait it out. Some families never seek professional help and consequently may never get outside confirmation that the disturbed person has a mental illness.

PHASE TWO: KEEPING THE PEACE

As early warning signs of the mental illness worsen, family relationships become increasingly fragile and disrupted.

Although families still do not grasp what's wrong, they begin to recognize that the changes in their loved one are serious and may be permanent. Shame and uncertainty prevent family members from reaching out for help. Instead they isolate themselves even further by staying home more and inviting company less.

They are living in a disturbed home environment yet no one is willing to discuss the problem because doing so would make them feel uncomfortable and might create more problems. Because of this lack of open dialogue, each one makes his own assumptions about the changes taking place. Some family members mistakenly assume that there is something wrong with them, when in fact, the disturbance is within another. When no one is discussing the problem, it is easy to make such assumptions.

Within their silence and isolation, families create unspoken agreements—the rules and expectations tacitly agreed to by family members, friends, and lovers, which are designed to keep the peace and to relieve the family of any more stress. Silent agreements made during this phase could be, "We won't talk about the bizarre changes in our father because they're only temporary," "Don't talk about your feelings so I won't feel compelled to talk about mine," or "Don't ask me what the problem is, I am not sure myself."

By this time, the ill person is often exhibiting pre-psychotic behaviors such as increased sleeplessness, absence of routine daily patterns, continued isolation, aggression, increased paranoia, suicidal thoughts, and hypersensitivity to others. Many begin living a private life made up of fictional figures, Mafia members, biblical characters, dead people, or famous individuals such as the President or rock stars. In the case of mania, euphoria and increased energy may also be present. When experiencing pre-psychotic behaviors, the individual is usually delusional and suspicious of others. Such delusions make it extremely difficult for the family to communicate with the ill person, increasing the isolation felt by the mentally ill person, who is also unable, or unwilling, to seek help independently, as the following example reveals:

> Jessica has two young children and a husband, Chris, who
> is unable to get out of the house to go to work. Since the
> death of his father two years ago, Chris has become
> depressed and withdrawn. Although he has not been hospi-
> talized, he frequently talks of suicide. He tells his children
> how to prepare for his death and what kind of funeral he
> wants. Jessica is frantic. Her trust money is running out and
> she hopes Chris will soon be able to return to work. She's
> thought of divorce but she would like to keep the family
> together. Yet she sees the worried looks on the faces of her
> children when their dad talks to them about death and
> funerals.

As the stress and disruption within the family intensify, its
members are forced to emerge from their silence and seek
ways to cope, to protect themselves from the increasing trouble and chaos. Still trying to keep the peace, some family
members will attempt to cure the ill person and in doing so
may get caught up in a variety of behaviors such as acting as
go-between within the family, or trying to be doctor, healer,
adviser, or therapist to the ill person. As a result, relationships
change from their natural, intended form of sibling to sibling,
child to parent, or parent to child, becoming "counselor to
client," or "doctor to patient." In may instances, child
becomes parent to the adults. The healthy member loses the
relationship he once had and takes on the role of rescuer.

Some family members choose another way to deal with the
escalating problems: they become uninvolved, seeking to
escape, to remove themselves from the chaotic home environment. This powerful coping mechanism is effective in helping
the individual insulate himself from conflict and disruption,
but is simply another form of keeping the peace. Social withdrawal and pretending to be unaffected by the surrounding
problems when in fact the person is angry and frightened are
forms of escape. Sometimes the choice of escape is danger-

ous, as with the abuse of alcohol or drugs. On the other hand, those who escape may find a healthy surrogate family in which they receive the stability and safety lacking in their own homes.

Families may remain stuck in this peace-keeping phase for months, years, or a lifetime. The family then never speaks honestly or openly about their thoughts and emotions. Although they may get together, they remain isolated from one another. The goal is to keep the peace, therefore, the truth is scapegoated into the background to keep everyone comfortable.

When the family continues to be isolated in this earlier phase, remaining silently divided, they are unlikely to receive outside help. It is important for families to understand how this can happen. With such insight, they may be able to seek professional help before they are forced to do so because of a serious crisis. A list of reasons why families may not seek professional help follows:

They are unable to discuss the problems together.

They lack the skills or resources it takes to reach out to one another.

They believe that problems should remain inside the family.

They are unaware of or deny a need for outside help because they have not yet identified the behaviors as symptoms of a serious mental illness.

They are reluctant to proceed without the ill person's cooperation, and the mentally ill person denies having a problem.

They disagree as to what needs to be done to help the person showing disturbed behavior.

They are reluctant to reach out for fear that such problems as physical or verbal abuse, alcoholism, or incest will be discovered.

The adults in the family prohibit seeking help because of other problems or abuses that exist in the family.

They fear seeking outside help because of the social stigma and blame.

Most families have lived through several psychotic episodes or crises before the first intervention by a professional. By not seeking help, they have allowed the mental illness to govern their lives.

A mother reveals why her family was unable to look for help: "I can't imagine now how we lived for ten years with Tom's mental illness without somehow getting help from someone. But I realize now we kept it our secret. Although we lived from one unpredictable disturbance to the next, the teachers at school, our neighbors, the rabbi, and our family physician never suggested that Tom may have needed psychiatric help. And none of us broke the silent agreement not to mention the unmentionable—that Tom has a psychiatric problem."

PHASE THREE: RUDE AWAKENING

As the disruptive behaviors persist, the family is pushed to the limit of its ability to live with ongoing crises and realizes that the ill person is not going to return to normal spontaneously. Threats of violence, sleepless nights, loss of appetite, hallucinations which are acted upon, inability to carry on a conversation, or a suicide attempt by the mentally ill person are behaviors that force the family to reach out to those with whom they have a trusting relationship. Typically, they first approach extended family members, neighbors, or friends with their concerns. After this, the family usually contacts physicians, clergy, or other authority figures. Unfortunately, relatives, friends, and nonpsychiatric professionals seldom offer information that improves the family's situation. This is due in part to the community's fear and ignorance of mental illness.

One woman describes how a physician she confided in sug-

gested she encourage her husband, who was later diagnosed as having a schizo-affective disorder, to have an extra-
marital affair: He claimed that her husband "sounds as if he
needs to sow a few wild oats . . . let off some steam." This
same woman also shared her problems with a friend. Her
friend advised that she keep her husband away from the
neighborhood children, and said the best thing would be
just to "keep him at home and wait it out."

Most families, already vulnerable, feel disgraced when they
reach out for answers. They feel discouraged, embarrassed,
misunderstood, feared, or blamed for causing the dis-ease.
The naive response by community members highlights the
social stigma that families encounter throughout the course
of the mental illness. This stigma simply perpetuates the isolation and secrecy within these families, and provides another
incentive to delay seeking some form of treatment.

Most families will have lived through the roller coaster of
unpredictable behavior and crises for years with no confirmation that the person has a mental illness. Then, when they
finally reach out for professional help, they are often met with
the cold reality of a physician's diagnosis. The family hears
that a loved one suffers from schizophrenia, manic-depression, or some other serious mental illness. The diagnosis is a
shock, although it confirms their suspicions and gives a name
to something that has baffled and frightened them. Yet their
sense of loss is usually greater than their sense of relief.

Simone is twenty-three and attends college in the same
town where her family lives. Just this past week her brother,
Matthew, was hospitalized. He hadn't eaten or slept for four
days, and he continued to pace up and down the hallway in
her parents' home, blurting out strange and frightening
comments about imaginary events. Simone's mother was
afraid to leave Matthew alone in the house. Finally, she
called the police and had Chris taken to the emergency
room at a hospital downtown.

Simone recalls her first visit to the hospital: "Matthew's doctor called a family conference. I expected to hear a progress report on Matthew's condition; I hoped to hear that my brother would be better soon—that the right treatment had been found for him, that he would be able to help me with my math assignments again. But when the doctor spoke he told us, 'Matthew is schizophrenic.' Tears clouded my view. My parents were dead quiet. I was nauseated. A sense of doom entered our lives that day. 'Matthew is schizophrenic,' he said, and asked if there were any questions."

The diagnosis brings with it a confirmation of the family's loss, an experience similar to that of a death. The original person—the one who was playful, ambitious, loving—has disappeared, replaced by someone who is unhappy, disruptive, and unpredictable. Families lose the relationship they had with that person before the illness along with the plans they shared and the many dreams for the future. The one with the mental illness experiences a loss, as well, that of the self he or she once was.

In addition to the loss of the original loved one, families of the mentally ill are confronted with a lifetime of losses: loss of other family members through emotional or physical withdrawal; loss when the mentally ill member is hospitalized; repeated loss as the ill person cycles between stability and illness; and, for some, loss through suicide. Adult children of parents who have a mental illness describe a childhood of losses and disappointments. Brothers and sisters describe the time their sibling started changing as a death, with the diagnosis as the confirmation from the coroner. Spouses often describe the onset of the illness as a time of abandonment and the end of what was once a supportive relationship.

In this phase, families may search desperately for the original person. They wait for the cause and, subsequently, for the cure to be found, for the miraculous reappearance of the loved one. Many families who appear to be searching for the cause of the illness are in effect searching for the original person. This search is similar to the denial of a death. It is necessary, in time, to accept that the person may never be as before. If families continue to search for the original person, or the cause of the illness, they are not accepting the illness, or the ill person as he is in the present. This denial is painful for everyone in the family, as the following story illustrates:

"Every Sunday night my family has a dinner where we exchange stories and share what our plans are for the coming week. Mark used to tell such grand stories of what he was learning in college and who he met. But since he got sick and spent a summer in the hospital, he sits quietly at the end of the table, his eyes focused on his plate, sometimes mumbling to himself. I once asked him to tell a story, but he got angry and left the table. No one talks about his summer in the hospital. No one asks him what his day was like or if he has plans for the week. But I keep going to our Sunday dinners hoping Mark will tell us another one of his stories, hoping this time Mark will look up at me and smile."

Families need to break the silent agreements that prevent them from talking about feelings or dealing with the loss openly. They need to learn to deal with conflicts and problems together.

Much research is dedicated to the effects loss has on one's personal development, especially when the loss occurs during childhood or adolescence. The loss of any close relative, such as a parent, sibling, or spouse, has profound effects on those remaining behind. Whether or not it is a positive or negative effect depends on how the family responds to such a loss. Loss is a natural part of life. We can't prevent loss; we can't guarantee that our loved ones will not have a serious dis-ease. Mental illness needs to be recognized as a major loss. The primary distinction between mental illness and death is that mental illness is not recognized as a significant loss, when, in fact, loss may be the primary trauma for family members during the course of the mental illness. Furthermore, families experience chronic loss because the ill person cycles between periods of stability (life) and periods of psychosis and instability (death).

The loss of someone who is diagnosed with a long-term mental illness such as schizophrenia seems final. Families fear nothing will ever be the same. Inside they weep over the brother who could play piano, the mother who used to read stories, the husband who enjoyed playing tag with the children. That person is gone now, perhaps forever. The family then loses sight of of what possibilities lie ahead through recovery, focusing instead on their loss.

Family relationships become strained when the focus is increasingly on the ill person. Most often, as the focus of the parents turns to the needs of the mentally ill child or spouse, other family members are given less attention. Parents find they receive less support from spouses. This lack of attention creates more losses experienced within these families. The high rate of divorce in these families may be due in part to the lack of attention a spouse receives as the other spends time taking care of the mentally ill son or daughter. Divorce then creates another major loss for the family to cope with.

With a diagnosis comes a prognosis, which in the case of most mental illnesses sounds bleak. Consequently, families prepare themselves for a lifetime of loss and crisis. Along with the prediction that the dis-ease is chronic—incurable—families begin to grieve chronically. Chronic grief leads to feelings of hopelessness, regret, and failure. Family members grieve for the past, regret mistakes they believe were made, and reluctantly consider their futures. This hopelessness quickly turns into helplessness.

Such silent grieving inhibits the search for solutions to family problems and can lead to an even deeper isolation among family members. Much like the family in which everyone knows Dad is an alcoholic but no one is talking about it, families of the mentally ill continue to submerge their feelings and concerns. Not talking about the mental illness generates a sense of hopelessness because neither feelings nor solutions are discussed. For example, if no one shares his concerns about Dad's drinking, the family is closed to possibilities of handling the problem. So it is with families of the mentally ill who do not openly mourn but grieve in silence. Denial, hopelessness and failure become the norm in these families.

In families in which a loved one has died, mourning allows them to grieve over their loss, to open up about their feelings, and finally, to accept their loss. Similarly, families of the mentally ill need time to mourn their loss, express their feelings, get comfort, and accept the illness. Mourning is simply a process of communicating the many feelings one has over a loss. Families need to foster an atmosphere in which mourning is encouraged.

Throughout the course of the dis-ease, the mentally ill family member also experiences loss. Individuals with mental illness may feel that they have lost much of their original personalities, as well as their goals, expectations, skills, behaviors, and relationships. They too need an environment in which mourning is permitted.

One mother tells how she gave up grieving over the loss of her "old" son: He was once an athlete and scholar. Now he is unable to accomplish many daily tasks that are easy for most people. Still hopeful, his mother waits for some sign that he will be able to finish school. Instead he continues to withdraw into his world of grandiose thinking and day dreams. She waited for his recovery for thirteen years, until her husband left the family and Nick attempted suicide. She admits that, "I tried my best to keep the family together, but nothing worked. I decided not to try so hard anymore." She went to the hospital and talked with her son while he recovered from his overdose of medication. She told him how his illness affected her, and that although she misses the old son, they both needed to accept that he had a very serious illness and that neither of them could be sure that he would ever completely recover. When she did this, they both cried, and her son said to her, "The old me is still in here, Mom." Her son then realized that he felt suicidal because he, too, remembered what he was like before he became ill with manic-depression. He had spent hours ruminating over his failures, hating himself for what he had become.

Another woman recalls how her life changed with the rude awakening; "My mother was always paranoid and critical of others. I don't remember it being any other way," says Sadie, now an adult child. "Now I realize she was trapped inside her mental illness, which was a complex web of delusions and suspicions. She was sexually abused by her grandfather and never given the opportunity to recover. For me, the rude awakening came during my own therapy, realizing my mother was a very ill woman. Soon after I realized she was mentally ill I joined an Eight Stage group and worked out my own pain around her abuse and neglect of me."

In time, the mental illness is no longer the primary cause of family problems, but rather how family members respond to the illness. The family is increasingly disrupted as, more and more, family members follow separate paths as they deal with the illness and their lives. Eventually, tragically, the family unit breaks down.

PHASE FOUR: JUST COPING

Rita and Kevin are the sister and brother of Richard, who is diagnosed as having paranoid schizophrenia. Richard began showing signs of his illness eight years ago, when he was fifteen. Rita explains: "It becomes a matter of survival. We have struggled through years of disappointment, and either you learn to survive or you begin feeling crazy yourself. Kevin and I chose to live together—three hours away from my mom and Richard. She calls us in a crisis, which is almost every week, and we take turns going home and mending things. Sometimes she just needs to talk to us over the phone. Kevin and I are fortunate because we have each other. My father died three years ago so my mother lives alone with Richard. We don't want Richard to live with her; we think he could make it in a board-and-care facility. The worst part, though, is I feel so guilty when I think of leaving my mom with Richard—and when I think of Richard, who used to be such a smart, happy person."

The ways in which family members responded to the initial crisis of the mental illness now become long-term coping strategies. Coping methods vary but are limited. As one fourteen-year-old daughter of a mentally ill mother says, "Yes, I'm coping! I stay away from my mother, I read a lot of science fiction, and I spend a lot of evenings at my boyfriend's house."

Furthermore, coping strategies may be destructive, as when someone uses alcohol to deal with pain and problems. When family members "cope" by engaging in denial, chronic grieving, giving up their own needs to care for others, and drug abuse, they become victims of the mental illness. After years of living with disturbances and unpredictable behavior, family members adopt these coping techniques to gain some control over their lives.

The home is supposed to be a refuge. But seldom is refuge found in these homes. Many families tell of their mentally ill loved ones acting out violent delusions and threatening them. While few incidences of actual violence are reported, many families live in fear of possible violence. Family members also have other fears which create an unstable environment. Those who have a sibling or a parent with a mental illness often fear that they too may become mentally ill. Some fear the possibility of having children who are mentally ill and live with a sense of hopelessness about their own futures. Getting away or drug use may help them cope with their fears by making it easier to deny them.

Donna's home is not safe. Both her mother and the youngest of her two sisters have a mental illness. Her mother was in and out of the hospital during the first five years of Donna's life. Her mother was a frightening woman who was unable to show family members any love. Donna's parents were divorced when her mother was pregnant with their third child, Marnie. Donna was five at the time. Marnie later was diagnosed with the same mental illness as her mother. By the time she was thirteen, Donna was a parent to two sisters and a mentally ill mother. Her mother somehow stayed out of the hospital although she was never quite well. When Marnie became ill, Donna began drinking to control her fear. By eighteen, Donna left to live in another state with a cousin.

In Donna's words, "I had to leave. It all became too much for me. My mom wasn't getting any better, and Marnie was getting worse. I thought if I stayed, I'd be next! When I got to Colorado, I really started to drink and smoke pot. I was so scared that I would soon be a schizophrenic, that I wouldn't be able to have children because it seems that mental illness is hereditary in my family. I also drank to quiet the guilt I felt at leaving my sisters and Mom. Although it was hell living at home, they are my family and I love them. I'm thinking of inviting Marnie to live with me now that I have quit drinking, but I don't know if I could handle it."

Typically, at least one person in the family copes by withdrawing. This avoidance is not to be confused with leaving to meet some personal goal such as attending school, beginning a life somewhere else or getting married. Those who withdraw to *cope,* also withdraw from *themselves,* avoiding their own feelings and goals. They withdraw into such negative behaviors as drug use or social isolation. On the other hand, a family member can remain in close contact with the family but continue to deny that his relative has a mental illness. This person will usually be emotionally unavailable, avoiding the family during a crisis involving the mentally ill loved one. Such avoidance, is simply a style of coping in a chaotic situation.

It's not that it's wrong to leave; in families where violence or abuse is a threat, it is wise to leave. However, when this response becomes a habit, alternative ways to handle such situations are overlooked. Until the person adopts new and healthier skills for dealing with conflict, this pattern of avoidance is blindly repeated in other relationships whenever conflict arises. Consequently, this way of coping becomes a pattern.

Advocating for better mental health services is another way families may cope. During this phase, family members may turn to advocacy when obtaining treatment is barred by obstacles such as stigma, ignorance, and lack of community services. Through advocacy, families organize to ensure better treatment for their relatives or to educate the public about the needs of the mentally ill. Their helplessness diminishes as they make positive changes by bonding together with other families of the mentally ill.

> A mother talks about her son: "He's home sitting on the couch smoking cigarettes all day. He only seems to be getting worse. I've tried getting him on several different medications and encouraged him to attend a local day program. But no matter what I try he just sits there day after day. There was no hope until I joined up with some other families who have a mentally ill son or daughter. I feel good when I'm with others who are trying to make life better for the mentally ill. I can't seem to help my son but perhaps I have the power to make some improvements for others."

Indeed, advocacy is a necessity if services are to improve for the families of the mentally ill and if the social stigma surrounding mental illness is to be eradicated. Advocacy can provide purpose and refuge for many family members. However, there is a danger that family members will use advocacy as a way to ignore the immediate family problems. For too many, improving the mental health system becomes more important than improving family relationships. Most often, those who are advocates are also involved in caring for the mentally ill person. In addition to concentrating on improving the mental health system, they focus on improving the life of the mentally ill relative. They try to gain control in their lives by controlling the mentally ill person or others, too often losing control of their own lives.

One of the roles of the family is often to be the primary provider for the family member with mental illness, who is often in need of others to care for him, and even dependent on others to make some of his decisions. When the mentally ill are psychotic or otherwise unstable, they are usually incapable of providing for themselves, sometimes even putting their lives and the lives of others in jeopardy. Often, families are expected to control their mentally ill relative if he is endangering himself or others. Because of this, there is a constant emphasis on the needs and problems of the mentally ill person and very often little thought is given to the needs of the family and its other members.

Families learn to cope with the tragedy of mental illness by making plans for the future care of their mentally ill relative. Understandably, parents are concerned for the future well-being of their mentally ill children, and they prepare for it as best they can. Most often, these plans include a sister or brother providing care for the mentally ill loved one. Parents may not be aware that how they care for their mentally ill loved one *now* sets the stage for the lives of the future providers—the siblings and adult children of the mentally ill. Silent agreements become oriented toward the future: "My ill daughter will live with one of her siblings when we are no longer able to care for her." "My husband and I will set up a trust fund with her siblings as guardians." "My time spent in advocacy will create services for my son's future." Too often, siblings and adult children of the mentally ill do not have the opportunity freely to choose to be the future providers. Instead the choice is made for them. Furthermore, those siblings and adult children who are the chosen future providers for the mentally ill are often ill-prepared for the task.

Jane's older sister, Katie, has epilepsy and severe depression. Jane has spent much of her teenage years looking after Katie. Wanting to be helpful to her parents, she did whatever she could to relieve their burdens. Jane is very knowledgeable about Katie's seizures, which she has as often as twice a week. Her doctors tell the family that not all Katie's seizures are physical in origin—some are psychological. They say Katie is trying to get attention. Jane sees only how Katie cries after each seizure. In fact, Katie cries a lot. Now, at seventeen, Jane is beginning to wonder about her own future. She is sure of only one thing—that Katie will be part of her plans.

Perhaps, like Jane, family members find it difficult to plan their futures without the mentally ill loved one in mind. Moreover, some feel guilty if they do not make plans to care for their mentally ill relative. However, many speak of being angry because the love and care they give to the mentally ill family member are not returned. The relationship between the mentally ill person and other family members is strained, yet the family continues to provide primary care. Later, siblings feel resentment as their lives are continually disrupted by the mental illness. The resentment is often suppressed because of guilt family members feel at having escaped being afflicted by mental illness. The guilt, in turn, is likely to remain unspoken.

Parents can unwittingly play into such feelings by expecting their healthy children to continue providing the kind of care to a mentally ill family member that they provided over the years. Furthermore, the style of caretaking is already designed for these future providers, as shown in this story:

Kathy, an adult sibling of twenty-five, tells of her concerns about her future role as her brother's provider: "My brother, Steve, has a schizo-affective disorder which is presently controlled by medication. He's been stable for a few months, the longest since his first psychotic break eleven years ago. But it is the future I am concerned about. Who will care for Steve when my parents no longer can? I am in my final year of college, and I want to move away and start a life of my own. But I feel awful leaving Steve with my parents. One time, he threatened to burn the house when they asked him to move out. So, out of fear, my parents let Steve live with them. They are also afraid he will just end up on the streets if they make him move out.

My other brother lives in another state and has no contact with the family. He is a successful attorney and claims he has no time for Steve's problems. Either I take care of Steve or he will end up in some state institution or on the streets. And I can't live with that either. I wish my parents would get Steve out of the house and into treatment; maybe then the future for him—and me—wouldn't look so gloomy."

For too many family members, especially the siblings and adult children of the mentally ill, caring for their mentally ill loved one is something that they feel they *should* do—an expectation precipitated by guilt.

Because families feel limited in how to cope with the mental illness, they often believe they are failures. But they have not failed; they have simply allowed certain unhealthy coping strategies to become habits. Families of the mentally ill must realize that there are many alternatives; that there are ways to care about a mentally ill loved one without further disruption of the family and without losing sight of one's personal goals.

PHASE FIVE: A DELICATE BALANCE

The question is not whether families *should* provide for their mentally ill loved one. It's good to extend love, respect, and to share resources with a family member in need. The question is *how* the family provides this care and how much of any one person's time is taken up by being responsible for someone else's life and emotional well-being. The question is not whether it is right or wrong to withdraw from the family, but *what* is causing so many to do so in order to cope. The question is not how the family made mistakes in the past, but what the family can do now to become healthy. What can the family do to mend what's broken? And, what is broken is family relationships.

Which silent agreements are perpetuating unhealthy family relationships? How can families who are using all their energy just to cope start to thrive? How can the silence and isolation between family members be ended? Regardless of the tragedy that the mental illness causes each family member, it is time now to recognize that there are alternative ways to handle the challenges—if the family is open to these new ways.

Gretchen, whose husband had depression and severe anxiety for fifteen years, tells this story of a man who had faith in God: "A flood hit this man's town with such severity that all were either washed away or given only a few hours to save themselves. The water quickly reached the stairs leading to his house. As he sat praying on his porch, a friend came by in a boat and said, "Come along with me or you'll drown." But the faithful man rejected this kind invitation, saying, "Thank you, but no. God will save me." Another hour passed, and the man prayed and prayed, knowing God would rescue him. He knew, in spite of all circumstances, that he would be saved. The water had now reached his roof. He was sitting on his roof when a distant neighbor came by in another boat and made the same offer, "The boat is crowded but we certainly have room for you. Come with us before the flood takes your life." And he replied again, "No, God will save me." Not too much longer, he was on his chimney and all that could be seen for miles was green water and a few other chimneys. As he sat there praying in earnest, another boat came by with a stranger in it. "Sir," the stranger called, "come in my boat and save yourself!" But again, the man resisted and stated, "God will save me." It was but moments later that this man found himself in heaven in the presence of God. Angrily the man said to God. "I prayed for you to save me, I believed in you! And you let me drown!" And God gently replied, "My son, I sent three boats after you and you rejected them all."

Family members who reach this phase are willing to take a look at alternatives and decide what they can do to improve their lives and the lives of their loved ones. They open up to the alternatives—the many boats life offers to handle the many challenges one encounters. They recognize that the coping skills they have learned can become self-defeating when they become habits. They know that in order to effectively care for someone else, they must first learn to understand and care for themselves better.

The remainder of this book is written to help family members move beyond the Just Coping phase, to create the Delicate Balance of caring for oneself while still caring about someone who has a mental or emotional illness. This is a workbook in that changes need to take place if family members want to create this balance. However, this is not a recipe book in which only certain ingredients will produce the desired results. Undoubtedly, there are many ways to improve the well-being of these families. This book is meant to suggest ways family members can learn to live beyond the disruption that the mental illness has caused; to care for others in a way which encourages personal dignity for everyone; to live productive and creative lives; to experience an inner calm in spite of chaos; and, most important, to live positively without guilt, shame or fear.

The Gift

If you had a gift
which was not received,
what would you do?
And if your gift was you
and you were not received,
then what would you do?
Would you say your name
to no response?
Maybe you'd say it louder,
then louder again,
and then begin to mutter.

Perhaps you would wander through
this world giving a false name,
giving people only what they ask for.
That wouldn't work after awhile.
So you'd write a poem
to the trees and to the stars
who never move,
who never say who they are,
who are either acknowledged
or not acknowledged.
But you would know them.

— JERE TRUER, MA, LICSW
Trainer for the Eight Stage Healing Process, Poet

2

You Can Heal Anything You Can Name

*Something we were withholding made us weak
Until we found out that it was ourselves.*
— ROBERT FROST

Of all the knowledge, the wise and good seek most to know themselves.
— WILLIAM SHAKESPEARE

STEPHEN

Stephen is a sophisticated and calm man of thirty-two. He is a talented, educated, and proud person. But Stephen is reluctant to let anyone close enough to him to discover that inside he feels insecure, nervous, and alone. It was with a friend that he finally opened up: "I am not doing well. I keep pretending I'm doing just fine. People depend on me to be all right. I've invested so much energy in convincing others that everything is okay with me, that I'm getting sick. I've been holding my feelings inside me for so long my doctor's finally named it—colitis. A fancy term for ulcers in my colon. I figured I had better do something to get my health back so I went to a therapist. I was talking to her about my family . . . you know my sister has schizophrenia and my father is an alcoholic. There seems to be a weak link in my family and I wonder sometimes about my own sanity. I wouldn't share this with anyone in my family. I sometimes wonder if I'm going crazy. There just doesn't seem to be any place for me to go for help. Maybe, having colitis, my feeling scared and angry inside is normal. Really, I'm just not sure what *normal* is anymore. The therapist suggested the Eight Stage group for me. I think I'd be dead if I hadn't followed her suggestion."

Stephen learned early to be a Caretaker. Up until now he has been so invested in being the healthy one, the one who is there for others, that he has lost the skills to take care of himself effectively. For Stephen it has become a habit to hold in his feelings of anger, anxiety, and grief. As an adolescent he was aware of his younger sister's mental illness. However, he never understood that his father's erratic and abusive behavior might also have been signs of an emotional illness. He was told that his father was an alcoholic, but the strange behavior continued long after he was sober. Because in Stephen's family "personal problems" have led to mental illness and alcoholism, to him being healthy meant showing no signs of personal problems. Stephen learned that emotions and inner conflict were danger signs of mental illness. Consequently, he believed he must keep his anger, anxiety, and grief to himself.

It wasn't until recently that Stephen began to explore his own mental health. He is determined to heal his colitis, to allow his feelings to surface and build a new life, with more balanced relationships.

KATIE

"I didn't know Katie for very long before she moved in with me. We met at school and agreed to rent a duplex together near campus. It wasn't until she was moving out five months later that I realized the depth of her problems. As she packed, I noticed that all her belongings had KIJ written across them. She had even marked her frozen food with her initials.

"Living with her was uncomfortable. She tended to isolate herself. She was never quite honest about what she wanted. She was never quite comfortable with herself or others. I knew she had had a traumatic adolescence, with mental illness in her family, but somehow it seemed crisis followed her everywhere. One issue or another, a broken relationship or some other conflict, created a drama from which she was constantly escaping. At first I thought she just had bad luck, that she just needed someone to care for her. But I couldn't give her the amount of attention she demanded. I came home one day and she simply stopped talking to me. She was getting ready to move out. I was willing to talk, to work things out, but I couldn't penetrate her secrecy and silence. Now I'm relieved she's gone. The house is more peaceful since she left."

Katie is an Escape Artist. Her life is filled with crisis, yet she never stays in one place or in one relationship long enough to resolve a problem. When the crisis is at its peak, she flees. Katie has become a victim of her own design, a victim of the past, which she repeats. She has become so accustomed to crisis that she often creates it. Her relationships are typically short-lived and end traumatically. She tends to attract people who support her belief that the world is unsafe and full of chaos, or people who will take care of her when she feels victimized. Her cycles of crisis are intertwined with long periods of isolation.

For Katie to end this cycle she will need to stop running

from conflict, which is a natural part of intimate relationships. She will need to learn that life can be exciting without crisis and problems. For Katie to bring balance into her life means an in-depth personal inventory of herself and her relationships.

LOUISE

Louise owns a small card shop in the Southeast. She has had two marriages end in divorce. To others she is the epitome of the organized, prosperous, productive single female in her mid-thirties. But Louise knows that she is not the superwoman she portrays herself to be. In reality, she feels awkward in a world where it appears to her that everyone else knows the secrets of happiness—that others are capable of intimate relationships while she is not. Because she is perfectionistic and judgmental in her attitude toward herself and others, she doesn't allow in the rewards offered her in relationships, and as a result, she isolates herself. Fearful of being alone the rest of her life, she believes she lacks the skills it takes to engage in a committed and intimate relationship.

When asked, she explains her divorces by saying: "I married for the wrong reasons." However, it is more complex. Both her husbands had significant personal problems. Both were raised in alcoholic and abusive families. "I didn't recognize either one's problems until after we were married. I am so accustomed to chaos and stress, I didn't heed the warning signs. Even when the small voice inside me nudged me to see the problems, I distrusted my intuition. Through counseling and the Eight Stage Healing Process, I recognized how mental illness in the family can set one up to be in abusive or neglectful relationships as an adult. I was seeking love and attention from men who were incapable of giving it to me. I wanted to believe that the attraction I felt was love, but what I was attracted to was what was familiar to me."

Louise exhibits the behaviors of a Caretaker and an Escape Artist. In fact, when she attempts to escape, it is often from her self-imposed responsibilities of caring for others. Through her marriages, Louise was searching for rescue, not companionship.

Louise's fantasies about being rescued began at a young age. When she was twelve, one of her brothers became ill, initially with agoraphobia. Later, he was diagnosed with schizoaffective disorder. Her father was absent during most of her life. At first, he traveled on business, later he stayed away to avoid the family. Her other three brothers abused marijuana and alcohol and her mother was preoccupied with caring for a large family and her mentally ill son. From her mother, Louise learned that "love is putting others first." As her mentally ill brother became increasingly disturbed and her family more disrupted, her escape was to fantasize. When real life did not produce a rescuer, she invented one. Most often they were the men in her life—boys, teachers, clergy, employers, husbands. This family environment taught her to "make-up" relationships, rather than see the reality. Because she grew up in a home where she adapted to the crises of mental illness, drug abuse, and neglect, engaging in a loving relationship is something she will have to learn as an adult.

Louise is ending her search for a rescuer. Her goal now is to find safety and love within herself. She is learning what love is . . . and what it is not. She now recognizes, through her personal healing process, that the commitment to love must first be made to herself.

Maybe you identify with Stephen, Katie, or Louise. Their stories are examples of behavior patterns learned within families with mental illness and are not uncommon. There are as many variations of such stories as there are people to tell them. Here are two more.

ALEX

Alex married at a young age. He was quickly attracted to Simone, whose mood swings entertained him. She was exciting and beautiful. It wasn't until seven years into their marriage and two children later, that Simone withdrew into a constant state of fear. Simone is often agoraphobic and paranoid. She distrusts everyone and feels safe only when she can lock the world out.

Alex is not interested in professional intervention for Simone. Instead, he places an ad in the local paper for someone to be his wife's "companion." The relationships with the hired companions last until Simone becomes suspicious of them. Alex believes his wife is "unique," and refuses to admit that her behaviors are symptoms of a disease. He chooses not to see the destructive effects of her behavior on the entire family. Financially, he can afford hired companions. But the cost to him and the family is far beyond monetary expenses.

MELODIE

Melodie loves her sister, Lisa. She wants to help her in every way she can. And Lisa needs assistance in the simple tasks of daily living. For instance, last night she called Melodie and asked if she could come over for dinner, since she was hungry and had run out of food stamps again. Even though Melodie prepared her sister's favorite dinner, when Lisa came over she hardly ate. At the same time, Melodie felt guilty because she was preoccupied with a term paper that was due in three days. Her sister does most of the talking during their visits anyway. As Melodie recalls, "She thinks I am treated better than her and she complains about this every time we are together. She mostly talks about how lucky she feels I am . . . having my own apartment and going to school. She is always commenting on how if she weren't mentally ill Dad would help her out more. She seems so bored and unhappy with her life—I try to make her happy, but nothing works. After her visits I feel so empty and sad. I feel as if there is something terribly wrong with me."

Each person is unique and each person's situation is different. Some people have painful and destructive experiences with the mentally ill. Others may experience less trauma and be less affected. Sometimes people learn to respond to mental illness openly and directly, without needing to escape or caretake. Each family member and friend of the mentally ill has his own story to tell, his own personal history, his own way of responding to the mental illness and family relationships.

Yet a common link exists among the lives of all family members and friends of the mentally ill. They are joined by their common experience of adapting to someone they care about who has a mental illness or serious emotional problem. But exactly how they adapt, how the mental illness affects them personally, may be different.

TAKING INVENTORY OF HOW YOU COPE

How have you reacted to the erratic, unpredictable, sometimes threatening behavior of a family member? How are you coping with the possibility that you may become the primary provider for a mentally ill relative? What fears and feelings do you secretly harbor? Also, what silent agreements have you made with your family in order to cope with the mental illness? What choices have you given yourself when dealing with the mentally ill person and other family members? In addition to his basic needs are you also involved with meeting the emotional, psychological, or spiritual needs of the mentally ill person?

Do you somehow escape from conflict? How has the mental illness affected your relationships with others in your life?

How has your family dynamic set patterns for you in your present relationships? Are your needs met within your many relationships? Does caring for others mean that their needs always come first? And how often does caring for others mean personal neglect? Are you now in an abusive or neglectful relationship?

Family members often feel trapped between their loyalty to, and guilty feelings about, the mentally ill. People in significant relationships with the mentally ill often wonder just how to love this person. A woman in therapy told how she coped with her father, who was schizophrenic. "I never answer the phone if it rings after 10 P.M." Although this might help her sleep at night and established boundaries between her and her father, her one coping skill didn't alleviate the guilt, worry, and anger she also spoke about so often.

Investigate your style of caring for others, your relationship to your mentally ill loved one, and how well you are taking care of yourself by reviewing the profiles that follow. Regardless of the distance between you and your mentally ill loved one, the mental illness has touched your life. These profiles will help you take a closer look at yourself, your relationships, and how you have responded to mental illness in a family member or friend. Can you find characteristics of yourself in them?

Since the beginning of any change and the key to finding solutions to your difficulties lie in asking yourself the right questions, the profiles offered here are tools for self-evaluation. Not all the statements will be true for you but each one may give you further insight.

The Caretakers

Caretakers are those who put others' wants and needs before their own. In fact, they have more definite opinions about what is best for others than about what is best for themselves. They receive their love and nurturing by rescuing or caring for others because that is when they feel appreciated.

They quickly learn to neglect their own needs at the expense
of meeting others' requests. They have difficulty saying no to
others. In most relationships, they are likely to be involved
with someone who needs caretaking (an Escape Artist or a
Victim). They are either dissatisfied with their relationships
because they are usually giving more than they receive or are
unable to maintain intimate relationships. Caretakers feel
responsible for the failings and troubles of others. They find it
difficult to end destructive relationships, empathizing with
the problems of the abuser.

As a Caretaker:

- I find it easier to be concerned for others than I do for
  myself.
- I am typically behind in the many tasks I have set for myself.
- I feel used by others.
- I let others place a lot of demands on me.
- I generally feel responsible for how others feel.
- I am often frustrated and angered by the behavior of
  others.
- I get upset when events don't go my way.
- I judge myself harshly.
- I often find myself talking about other people's problems.
- I have given up my belief in a Greater Power/God, now
  believing I must solve my problems on my own.
- I can't seem to get involved in or maintain intimate rela-
  tionships.
- I attend family gatherings most often high on alcohol or
  other mood-altering drugs.
- I think no one understands how I feel.
- I am often worried about the future.
- I have considered professional counseling for myself but
  can't find the time for it.
- I believe that if I had done something differently the men-
  tal illness/family problems would not have been as serious.
- I fear I too may be mentally ill but do not share this fear

with others.

- I consider the problems of the mentally ill individual more significant than mine. Consequently, I do not bring up my own concerns with other family members.
- I am afraid of my own emotions because I have seen my mentally ill relative/friend lose control of his emotions. I believe intense emotions are a sign of mental illness and that it is dangerous to openly express one's emotions.
- I believe I could improve the family's problems if only everyone would do as I suggest regarding the mentally ill person.
- I have canceled plans, sometimes major ones, like attending college or moving, because of my relative/friend.
- I have canceled numerous social plans to care for my mentally ill relative/friend or to respond to a crisis.
- I focus more attention on the mentally ill individual during a family or social gathering than I do on myself. For example, after leaving a family gathering, I more easily recall how he behaved, didn't behave, or felt than what I got out of the experience.
- I tend to be the one who initiates discussion of issues regarding the mentally ill relative/friend with other family members.
- I assume a primary role in the care of my mentally ill relative/friend.

Caretakers as People Pleasers

Caretakers are often Pleasers—Pleasers will go to almost any lengths to please others in order to get others to accept them. Not only do they put others' needs first, they value others' opinions and feelings more than their own. They care about what others think of them but do not think of themselves as valuable. Their main concern is to receive recognition and love through pleasing others. People typically become pleasers after years of caretaking or after years of living with a family where such behaviors are rewarded.

As a Pleaser:

- I find it very difficult to say no even when I feel I want to.
- I do not get angry with others even when there may be cause to.
- I avoid talking about my own concerns and problems.
- I apologize for my behavior and my feelings.
- I feel a need to be accepted by everyone around me.
- I form relationships in which I desperately seek the other's approval and love.
- I feel anxious and fearful that I may not receive love or appreciation from others.
- I seek approval from others rather than making choices on my own.
- I lie to others in order to be accepted.
- I often find myself the go-between in others' arguments/conflicts.
- I have kept the mental illness and other family issues a secret, even from those I trust most.
- I feel selfish when I attempt to put myself first.
- I am easily manipulated by others.
- I panic when someone ends a relationship with me.
- I feel something is terribly wrong with me.
- I have thoughts and images about being sexually abused.

Caretakers as Codependents

Codependency is a reliance on people and circumstances outside oneself, along with a serious neglect of oneself. It is an over involvement with the problems of another. Codependency is now viewed as a dis-ease in itself because it disables people. Those who are disabled by codependency rely on others for love and acceptance but do not love or accept themselves. They constantly need others to fill up the emptiness they feel inside.

As a Codependent Caretaker:

- I focus my attention on how others think, feel, and behave but am confused when it comes to my own feelings, thoughts, and behavior.
- I am much clearer about what others want from me than what I want from them.
- I blame myself when a relationship doesn't work.
- I invest a lot of energy in mending wrongs.
- I tend to go from one unhealthy relationship into another because I must be in a relationship with someone.
- I anticipate others' needs.
- I am attracted to needy people.
- I find needy people are attracted to me.
- I find I am bored or feel worthless when I don't have a problem to solve.
- I believe my self-worth is dependent on what others think of me.
- I can't end relationships with people whom I don't like or who are not good for me.
- I search for happiness and love outside of myself.
- I ask for love from people who are incapable of intimacy.
- I rationalize neglecting my own needs because I am too busy working or worrying about others.
- I find it difficult to share what I think or feel.
- I try to earn love from others by being successful, clever, etc.
- I often feel trapped in my relationships.
- I doubt that I will ever experience a nurturing relationship.
- I feel frustrated, angry, or hurt when interacting with my mentally ill relative/friend because he does not do what I believe is in his best interest.
- I feel personally responsible for the emotional well-being and care of my mentally ill relative/friend.
- I believe the family should be responsible for the mentally ill relative regardless of what sacrifices are required.
- I feel exploited by my mentally ill relative/friend but

choose not to do anything about it because I believe the mentally ill cannot be held accountable for themselves.
- I feel defensive when others suggest I spend too much time involved in my family's problems.
- I am scared/hesitant to ask for what I want in a relationship for fear of being denied or rejected.
- I'm not sure how to set limits with others; I am confused about what limits I have a right to put on others.

Escape Artists

The Escape Artists, for the most part, are invisible to others. They have learned to deal with the stresses in their lives through escape and isolation. Their choices of escape assume many forms, including the use or abuse of mood-altering drugs. Excessive fantasizing, denial, avoidance, and compulsive behaviors, such as unnecessary shopping, are other forms of escape. Generally, Escape Artists feel lonely but can act as if they are happy and secure.

Escape Artists quickly learn as children or young adults that being comfortable means being detached and uninvolved. Often, they remain uninvolved with their parental family, stepping back and letting others take charge. Often times, parents create Escape Artists through their neglect. The tragedy for the Escape Artists is that they continue to "escape" relationships, emotions, and conflict throughout their lives. They become invisible. Sadly, their lives too often become a cycle between inviting and avoiding crisis, as was described in Katie's story earlier in this chapter. They are experts at hiding their feelings and use denial as a tool to avoid conflict or exposure. Often they are involved with a Caretaker or someone who won't expect them to reveal themselves emotionally. Typically, they may go to others for intimacy only to withdraw from the relationship prematurely. Overall, it is the Escape Artists who are least likely to get help or admit the influence that the mental illness has on them and their relationships. Overall, Escape Artists learn to cope by escape or invisibility.

As an Escape Artist:

- I may have ulcers, headaches, or difficulty breathing.
- I get upset when others change their minds.
- I may have an eating disorder.
- I use alcohol or other mood-altering drugs more than three times a week.
- I abuse alcohol or other mood-altering drugs to the point where they interfere with my relationships with others.
- I cannot attend a family gathering without being high on alcohol or some other mood-altering substance.
- I have lost my faith in a Greater Power/God.
- I am often uncertain as to how I feel.
- I am reluctant or uninterested in seeking professional help for myself.
- I can't seem to set personal goals.
- I believe that my changing for the better will not positively affect the difficult relationships I seem to have with others.
- I am afraid of my own emotions because I have witnessed my mentally ill relative/friend lose control. Furthermore, I believe emotions are a sign of weakness.
- I am upset with my family but would never let on about my thoughts/feelings.
- I fool others into believing I have no concerns with regard to the mental illness but this is a lie.
- I isolate myself.
- I am not convinced that mental illness affects family members.
- I believe that the only thing that will improve the mentally ill individual's problems is the right medication.
- I have little or no involvement with my family.
- I let others in the family provide for the mentally ill relative.
- I find it easier to avoid conflicts.
- I am often told that I am "mysterious."
- I am sarcastic.

- I fear my own feelings.
- I set rigid rules for myself and others to follow. Or, I have no rules or limits.
- I don't know what is expected of me in intimate relationships.
- I fear what may be expected of me in intimate relationships.
- I am secretive.
- I have lied to others to avoid opening up.
- I distrust others more often than I trust them.

Isolation is one of the great escapes. There are many clever ways to isolate and keep ourselves shut off from others, and ultimately from ourselves. Generally, isolation is what the Escape Artist accomplishes through all his negative behaviors such as drug abuse, distrust, not reaching out and risking intimacy with others. The added problem is that no one can heal in isolation. To heal, to mend what is broken, we must come out of isolation and open ourselves up to others in an intimate way.

Escape Artists as Victims

Because of their inability to take care of themselves, Escape Artists are often Victims. Victims feel abused and misunderstood by others. They rarely, if ever, experience satisfying relationships. They feel needy but lack the skills to get these needs met, finding it difficult or even impossible to ask for what they want for fear of ridicule or rejection. Often, they are in relationships where they are either abused or neglected. In fact, abuse and neglect feel normal to them. They don't like themselves much and consequently do not open themselves up to receiving love and intimacy from others. Typically, Escape Artist/Victims relinquish themselves to others' demands, withdrawing more and more into a loneliness that to them feels impenetrable.

As a Victim:

- I find that my life feels unstable.
- I may be in a relationship where I am emotionally, physically, or sexually abused.
- I feel victimized by others.
- I tell myself I can't do anything right.
- I feel a lot of guilt but am not sure why.
- I often fantasize about suicide or have attempted suicide.
- I think nothing will ever work out for me.
- I can't seem to make good choices.
- I am scared a lot.
- I feel deprived of love and appreciation from others.
- I don't believe I am truly lovable.
- I believe that any abuse I experienced as a child was my own fault.
- I am angry about the attention the mentally ill person receives but would never share this with my family.
- I feel like a family outcast.
- I settle for relationships with people who neglect me.
- I just want someone to take care of me.
- I feel a lack of control over the direction my life is taking.
- I live in a state of fear.
- I don't believe my problems are important in comparison with those of the mentally ill relative/friend.

Escape Artists as Codependents

Escape Artists also have a propensity toward codependent behaviors. Codependency is a result of low self-esteem. Codependents rely more and more on others for love, acceptance, and worth, because they are incapable of giving this to themselves. As codependents, they are trapped behind a facade that says to others, "I am all right," when inside they are in pain. Whereas Caretakers who are codependent are more likely to be in a relationship with others who have problems or addictions, Escape Artists have addictions themselves, such as workaholism, compulsive spending, overeating, or alcoholism. Ultimately, the life of the Codependent/Escape Artist is out of control.

As a Codependent Escape Artist:

- I blame myself for most everything that goes wrong and don't see any way out of my problems.
- I disbelieve or distrust other's compliments.
- I feel inadequate in comparison with others.
- I expect rejection.
- I find it often takes a problem or crisis to motivate me.
- I find I am often reacting to the problems of others.
- I take others' behaviors and attitudes very personally.
- I am often overwhelmed by problems, especially those that involve others.
- I am afraid of making mistakes.
- I am uncomfortable if my projects are not perfect.
- I find it difficult to make decisions without the approval of others.
- I receive temporary and artificial feelings of self-worth by helping others.
- I appear rigid to others but am truly scared inside.
- I have a terrible fear of other people's anger.
- I am afraid or deny my own feelings of anger.
- I feel a crisis is always about to explode.
- I feel powerless in most, if not all, relationships and situations.
- I continue in relationships which are dead or destructive, while remaining emotionally detached.

Everyone will identify with some of these characteristics. Many of you may find yourselves thinking most of these describe you. Do not get discouraged. These are characteristics you learned in order to cope and survive in your family environment. They are not who you are. The truth of who you are will be found beneath the scar tissue of these characteristics. The important thing is that now you can begin to deal with your challenges because you've identified them. You can't change anything if you can't name it. Through the continued process of self-awareness and dedication to strengthening yourself and your relationships, you will begin to create that delicate balance that goes into a peaceful and fulfilled life.

BEGIN HERE, BEGIN NOW

Behaviors become self-defeating when they rob you of opportunities to experience the joy and nurturing that are available to you. You have the power to stop engaging in any of these self-defeating behaviors, if you so choose. Of course, it is not easy to free yourself from behaviors that are not only familiar, but have in some way been connected with your survival. Therefore, you are not expected to let go of any behavior or characteristic unless you identify it as self-defeating, and until you find another behavior to replace it.

Personal transformation is much like spring cleaning a home. You clean your home to be free of dirt and clutter. In order to make room for the new chair you want to put in your living room, you need to make a place for it. If you simply add furniture to your house without cleaning anything out, you will soon find yourself cramped and overcrowded. Do you really need to keep that old wicker chair with its wobbly leg? Similarly, you will find yourself confused and overwhelmed if you try to behave differently without first freeing yourself of the beliefs and feelings that keep you stuck in the old behaviors. The Eight Stages are designed to help you transform your relationships. Do you really want to stay in that relationship where you are neglected, abused or bored? First find the old, unhealthy ideas that need throwing out. Admit to yourself that these attitudes are self-defeating and then make room for the new by discarding the old (Stages 3, 4, and 5).

Family members often possess characteristics of both the

Caretaker and the Escape Artist. Another common pattern is for families to become divided into two camps: the Caretakers and the Escape Artists. Fortunately, within each family member there is a Caregiver waiting for the opportunity to express himself. The Caregiver frees himself from the self-defeating characteristics of the Caretaker and Escape Artist, making room to form mutually satisfying relationships with anyone—including the relative or friend with mental illness. He opens himself up to the well of creativity, self-worth, and love that has been buried within him.

The Caregiver: Creating That Delicate Balance

Caregivers take care of themselves first even while they provide support and nurturing to others. They extend love, resources, and ideas to others without jeopardizing or neglecting their own needs. Through self-awareness and commitment to a healing process, they have consciously decided to take responsibility for their lives and relationships. When conflict arises, they do not try to control it through manipulation or avoidance. Caregivers are able to end relationships that are a threat to their psychological, spiritual, or physical wellbeing. Finally, through a conscious effort, Caregivers create that delicate balance of caring for themselves while living with the reality of mental illness in a friend or family member.

As a Caregiver:

- I am aware that the family's problems have had an influence on me but have separated myself enough to meet my own needs.
- I am comfortable with the variety of emotions I experience-and share my emotions with those whom I choose to trust.
- I understand much of what a loving, supportive relationship consists of. Consequently my relationships are mutually satisfying.
- I have friends that I trust.

- I am an active part of a community.
- I continually do a personal inventory of my feelings, thoughts, and behaviors and leave others to do their own personal inventories.
- I take time each day to meditate/reflect or work on the Eight Stage Healing Process.
- I know I am ultimately responsible only for my own emotional well-being.
- I do not attempt to control others' behaviors.
- I am honest with myself and others.
- I set realistic goals for myself.
- I am able to release the need to control others and believe that there is a Greater Power/God that is benevolent, to whom I relinquish control.
- I do not blame others for my troubles.
- I am comfortable saying no.
- I do not engage in destructive relationships.
- I know I can love someone who is in trouble without feeling personally responsible for him.
- I invite others to be honest with me.
- I look forward to what the future holds for me.
- I am able to receive love, and compliments from others.
- I am focused on my thoughts, feelings, and behavior, not on others.
- I have the energy and time to be creative.
- I am compassionate without getting caught up in the problem myself.

You can choose to be a Caregiver whether you are the friend, parent, spouse, sibling, cousin, or adult child of a mentally ill person—you can enjoy your life and all your relationships. What is most important is that you first identify the behaviors or relationships that are obstacles to experiencing balanced, healthy relationships (stages 1,2 and 4), and then decide what you want to do (stages 3 and 8). Each person is responsible for himself. Identifying your self-defeating habits is the first step toward taking better care of yourself.

3

The Caretakers

You have made me a keeper of vineyards, yet my own vineyard I have not kept.

— SONG OF SOLOMAN

The phone rang at 3 A.M. Her first response was to ignore it because it was probably a crank call. When she did answer, it took a moment to identify the familiar voice.

". . . Your son is standing under the streetlight, Marge," he said.

"What? Who is this?" she asked.

"John . . . your neighbor. Marge, David is standing under the streetlight without a stitch on."

"What? Oh, my God, is he still there?"

"Yes, I can still see him standing there. He's just as still as death and looking up at the light. I thought we should call you, it's forty degrees out there. Donna wondered if we shouldn't call the police or something. I thought it best we call you."

"Right. Ahmm, thanks. Jack and I will take care of it. Christ! Okay John, thanks, bye."

Marge wakes her husband and in the process of trying to get David in the house the other three children are awakened. The crisis begins. They gaze at each other, wondering what to do, wondering what to expect and whom to call for help this time. The last time they tried to get him into the hospital for treatment he threatened to burn the house down when he got out. But he isn't being helped at home, not as sick as he is. Three in the morning quickly turns into 8 A.M., time for the other family members to deal with their own lives of high school, work, and day care. But it's hard to carry on the activities of a normal day when something so tragic looms over you. For Marge, her day includes explaining to John and Donna, her neighbors for twenty years, that her son David is mentally ill.

CARETAKING IS A CALLING

Families of the mentally ill are accustomed to meeting the needs of others in a crisis. In these families, caretaking becomes an expected role. The husband who denies he is mentally ill but refuses to go outside the house, the brother who believes he plays lead guitar for the Stones, and the mother who stays in her room all day all create a home environment in which there is a serious lack of stability and a demand for Caretakers. As the Caretaker will explain, "Someone has to step in and handle these unusual situations, extend a hand to the one in need." However, Caretakers do more than extend a hand. Because their world is so unstable and disordered, they invest a lot of time and emotional energy trying to get things back to normal.

When home life is chaotic, certain family members work at making the home environment tolerable for themselves. In an environment of peculiar, unpredictable, sometimes life-threatening behaviors, one often learns to survive by becoming a Caretaker. When the home is not safe, family members will create ways to protect themselves. Siblings and adult children of the mentally ill learn that in order to be safe they must caretake—they must take some control over their environment.

The problem is that the family Caretakers continue the rescuing and caretaking in relationships and circumstances where it is not necessary. The caretaking skills adopted in childhood and adolescence reappear in future intimate relationships, since we tend to repeat in our adult relationships what we learned in our families of origin. A Caretaker eventually feels responsible for others even during noncrisis times. Soon, caretaking responses become habits, as the following two examples illustrate.

Thirty-five-year-old Peter is a Caretaker when it comes to his brother Vance. Vance has schizophrenia and at this point there are no signs of recovery. In his support group, Peter described how he feels guilty when Vance reminds him that, "I'm mentally ill, I have no money, you're the only one who really cares about me." Although Vance lives in his own apartment across town from Peter, he visits Peter every day. Usually his visits are uneventful; he sits on Peter's couch, smokes cigarettes, and watches TV, sometimes listening to the stereo.

Peter hesitates to tell Vance to find another place to hang out because Vance is so lonely and has gotten in so much trouble with other people. Yet Peter lacks any social outlet of his own and doesn't see how he could invite a friend, let alone a date, over to his apartment. Peter feels harassed but doesn't know of any alternatives. After all, as he puts it, "Vance depends on me."

John, a father of three, describes his concern for his children, all of whom feel responsible for their mentally ill mother: "My wife has been sick for twenty years. Our children are grown up now; only the youngest, Becki, remains at home. We have all taken care of my wife. She has been in every treatment program imaginable, spending at least two months in the hospital every year. I am desperately concerned about the children. One of our children is away at college and I can tell by her letters that she is concerned about her mother and sisters. The youngest daughter asked me the other day if I want her to continue living at home after high school. I wanted to say, 'Yes, stay and keep your old dad company. Help Dad take care of Mom.' Instead I told her, no, she must move out on her own. I told her I can take care of everything at home. I wonder, though, if any of us can really live our own lives."

SELF-NEGLECT

The more involved you become in rescuing others, the more you are apt to neglect yourself. Self-neglect is characterized by an inability to set personal goals or maintain intimate relationships, abuse of alcohol or drugs, going against one's own wishes or beliefs to please others, or ignoring one's own feelings. Most Caretakers are experts at self-neglect.

Because Caretakers focus their attention on others' needs, they can go a long time neglecting their own. Taking care of others provides them with feelings of comfort, safety, self-worth, and stability. But it is a false security because caretaking is at the expense of one's own mental and spiritual health. This pattern of self-neglect is often repeated until alcohol or other addictions, problems with work, and other personal impasses finally force a person to take care of himself.

The major difference between Caretaking behaviors and Caregiving behaviors is what motivates our actions. We can ask ourselves, what is the motivation behind my "caring" behavior? Is is to keep the peace at any price, control someone? Is my motivation because I assume things will work out badly if I do not intervene? Or, is my motivation to benefit all involved (including myself), with an understanding of my limits?

One mother relates how it wasn't until her husband asked for a divorce that she began to take another look at her life: "I spent the last six years trying to get my daughter into treatment. She would be in one place and either do something to break their rules or run away. I ended up traveling to three different states to drop her off or pick her up. My husband is a professor at a large university and was doing okay with taking care of the other three children. They're all teenagers. But this fall I came home from touring another treatment facility to find my sick daughter had taken a Greyhound bus to California in an agitated, manic state. And my husband was asking for a divorce! It seems he's been wanting one for the past three years.... I realized then I no longer had control over my own life. I had even lost touch with my other children, whom I had all but forgotten for the past six years."

The above story illustrates the futility of caretaking. Your attempts to rescue, provide for, protect, and control others, especially when others have their own agenda, will result in self-neglect and a breakdown of other relationships. You cannot invest most of your time in "caring" for another person and expect to have your own life in order.

The following tale shows how caretaking can lead to self-neglect:

Rachel is an exceptional gardener. Somehow she is able to plant the same seeds as others in ordinary soil with magical results. Her garden is surrounded by a row of cooking herbs that gardeners with the best soil conditions grow with little success. Rachel's neighbors envy her talent. They soon ask her to teach them to plant a garden that produces such beautiful flowers, hearty vegetables, and exotic herbs. It starts out with a few requests but soon she is helping everyone plant and maintain their gardens. She feels special helping others. In fact, her popularity seems to be as endless as the seeds she plants. One day she comes home to her own garden to find the few vegetables that are there are small and full of worms. No herbs border her garden because she didn't have the time to plant them. The flowers that are left after the neighbors picked through the limited supply of seeds are not as beautiful and most are hidden by weeds. Her garden has not survived her neglect.

Depression in Caretakers

Depression in Caretakers is quite common. Depression is most often a sign that old patterns of coping with one's life and problems is no longer effective. Depression manifests from months or years of hopelessness and struggle.

When repeated efforts of rescuing and intervention seem futile, one begins to give up hope. When we try to open up to intimate relationships without adequate skills, our attempts result in more pain. We get stuck in a cycle of old behaviors accompanied by feelings of hopelessness and helplessness. After this pattern repeats itself enough times, depression occurs as a painful sign that we need to discover a new way to approach our lives and our problems. This is the value behind stage three: accepting that we cannot control anyone else's behavior and that we are ultimately responsible for our own emotional wellbeing.

FOSTERING UNNECESSARY DEPENDENCY

Everyone occasionally agrees to do or give more than he can handle, and the friends and relatives of the mentally ill are no exception. For Caretakers, however, setting limits becomes an especially painful dilemma. Caretakers find it difficult to act contrary to the needs of their mentally ill relative or friend, even when these needs run counter to their own. Unaware of what they can and cannot afford to give, they end up giving more than is necessary or healthy.

Initially, caretaking itself is an attempt to set limits. The Caretaker steps in to pick up the pieces after a disaster with the intention of limiting its impact on his life, or seeks to provide a sense of limits that the mentally ill person lacks. After all, a manic, psychotic, or suicidal person is generally unable to set his own limits. He is having enough trouble distinguishing illusion from reality.

However, the Caretaker goes too far in doing for the mentally ill person what he is able to do for himself. By constantly making decisions for him, the Caretaker protects him from the consequences from which most people learn. For example, after a psychotic episode or a suicide attempt, there may be something the mentally ill individual can do to prevent another such crisis, or at least to prepare to handle it better if it were to occur again. Perhaps he can gain some insight into why the crisis occurred or learn to recognize the warning signs. If families respond to crisis by protecting the loved one from understanding the problem and its consequences, he will not learn for himself but will come to depend on others as his buffer against reality. And the Caretaker rather than the mentally ill person will continue to endure the consequences. People who are mentally ill have idiosyncrasies and irritating habits just like anyone else, and these should be considered separately from their dis-ease. Mental illness does not automatically excuse someone from all responsibility. In addition, there are many behaviors that are not symptoms of the mental illness and need not be tolerated. Troubling behaviors may be ill-chosen coping strategies or may have been learned before the onset of the mental illness.

Terri's brother, Herb, has schizophrenia: Herb lives much like a street person. He easily fends for himself. In fact, he has a daily routine which includes visits to certain places, panhandling, eating out, somehow getting money to purchase the marijuana he smokes daily, actually buying the marijuana after he has made the proper connections, and socializing with other street people and merchants at the places he visits. He uses his welfare money to buy marijuana or for payment of his debts. When he runs low on money he will steal from his own family in order to get what he wants.

This same man, however, refuses to attend a vocational program where he could learn job skills, complains that others in the family have more opportunities than he does, and justifies his inability to do volunteer work by saying it is beneath him and coworkers make him paranoid. Although he has a high IQ, he excuses himself from taking a high school equivalency exam. This man has good interpersonal skills, is able to manipulate his environment and others quite effectively, knows how to provide for himself on the street, and engages in an active social life.

Herb's behavior demonstrates skills that could be used to enhance his life rather than to live it so tragically. His family members abuse drugs and alcohol, so they are unlikely to challenge his drug habit. As long as he is not psychotic, violent, or in danger, they assume he is okay. In reality, he is dying of cirrhosis of the liver, primarily due to abusing alcohol in combination with his medication.

Caretakers, in their role as protectors and rescuers, often lose sight of the actual capabilities of the mentally ill person. They are more attentive to how they think events should go and become more involved in controlling the outcome than in considering alternatives and involving the mentally ill person in decision-making. Often times, they don't want to "rock the boat" by taking risks and trying something new. In addition, with the family's continued focus on the disabilities of the person, the individual's capabilities are often overlooked. As demonstrated in the above example, Herb's street life shows his range of skills and manipulative powers, many of which could be used in a treatment program.

Fifty-seven-year-old Joanne lives with her brother, who has

been diagnosed with schizo-affective disorder. No one is quite sure of her brother's abilities because he has always lived with his family. "My parents always took care of my brother. The few times they attempted to get him into any treatment program he refused to go. Sometimes he would threaten to kill himself. My parents feared that he would live like an animal on the street and he has such a fear of strangers. When my father died I moved in with my mother to help take care of Frank. Now, four years after my mother died, Frank and I live together in an apartment overlooking downtown Cincinnati. He refuses any help and screams obscenities out the window at passersby. Frank is unwilling to live anywhere else and I can't leave him alone, can I? I go to work everyday and come home to Frank. I even fear leaving him alone for too long, so I don't go on many trips. He is getting more aggressive and I must admit I wonder if I will ever be in any danger from him. He's such a big man."

Sometimes the stress of setting limits and encouraging independence seems more difficult than taking care of someone. In the following example, a mother chooses to avoid stress and conflict by allowing her daughter Sandy to live at home instead of on her own. It is as much for her own peace of mind as for her daughter's safety that she encourages her daughter to live with her.

As Sandy's mother says: "She is incapable of taking care of herself! She is very vulnerable and was raped when she first attempted to live on her own. She would let almost anyone into her apartment and forget to lock the door when she went out. The neighborhood she lived in was unsafe but was all she could afford with her disability check. Besides, she's thirty-five and has lived with me most of her life. She shares the household chores and is an excellent cook. She's safest here with me. It's not perfect, she sometimes roams the house at night and doesn't get out enough. But she can't fend for herself out on her own and I can't handle her getting hurt again. I hope my other children are willing to take care of Sandy when I no longer can."

We might ask, how many of Sandy's dependencies were developed in the many years she lived with her mother? If Sandy can keep house and prepare meals, can't she learn to lock her apartment door? Are there safer neighborhoods or a program available to Sandy where she can learn independent living skills? Is Sandy's mother willing to set limits and insist that Sandy attend a program where she can learn to live on her own?

Caretaking is often passed down from one generation to another. In the above case, the mother assumes that one or all of her other children will take care of Sandy when she no longer can. Furthermore, they are expected to care for Sandy in the same way that her mother has chosen: by providing a home for her.

Dictating another's limits in order to prevent discomfort or a crisis is not a solution. And this is a catch-22 for families: they protect the mentally ill from the consequences of their behavior, which prevents the mentally ill from learning. As a result, families find themselves in a similar crisis again. They need to acknowledge that much of their rescuing and protecting is for themselves and not necessarily for the mentally ill loved one. Furthermore, rescuing is only a temporary solution and valuable only when others are in a life-threatening situation.

Granted, the mentally ill usually have a lower tolerance for stress than the rest of us. But the only way to assess someone's stress tolerance is to let him experience his own limits. Thus, the level of need and care should be individualized and evaluated throughout the ill person's lifetime. As he adapts to his disability, he should be encouraged to take more risks. The well person then is in the position to help the disabled person work toward independence rather than to encourage dependence. People with mental illness can learn their stress levels and how to maintain a stable environment while still achieving some level of autonomy. They can become effective at identifying the warning signs of a personal crisis and plan how to deal with increased feelings of anxiety, paranoia, or depression. But too often Caretakers are reluctant to allow such freedom.

The Caretaker can be compared to the "enabler" in an alcoholic family. People who become overinvolved in helping or taking care of the alcoholic are Enablers. They support the alcoholic behavior by protecting the alcoholic from experiencing the consequences of his destructive behavior. Ironically, it is out of love that people enable. The Enabler believes he is protecting the alcoholic from danger or humiliation, but this kind of love is harming thousands of people because it supports their alcoholism. Enabling has some parallels in families of the mentally ill. While it is less common for family members to "enable" mental illness, they do enable *dependency* by an unwillingness to set limits on their caretaking.

The Caretaker typically puts up with far more abuse, hostility, and ingratitude than others would tolerate in a relationship. Fulfilling demands because of threats like "I will kill you, burn down the house, live on the street" only perpetuates further dependency. Threats, after all, are a form of manipulation; through his threats the mentally ill person intends to get you to meet his demands. If you respond to such threats, you have tacitly agreed to this style of interaction and you can expect the manipulative and abusive behavior to continue.

COMPASSIONATE RESPONSIBILITY

"What is the purpose of life? I believe that satisfaction, joy and happiness are the ultimate purposes of life. And the basic sources of happiness are a good heart, compassion, and love. If we have these mental attitudes, even if we are surrounded by hostility, we will feel little disturbance."

— H.H. THE DALAI LAMA

I return the focus of my life to myself by appreciating my own worth, despite what may be going on around me.

— STAGE SEVEN

Because of their loyalty and devotion to the mentally ill loved one, Caretakers believe they are compassionate. After all, they think, "There but for the grace of God go I." But they are mistaking guilt for compassion. This so-called "compassion" is why the Escape Artists often feel ashamed. They believe others in the family are compassionate while they are not. On the other hand, the Caretakers feel burdened and angry because they think the Escape Artists are avoiding responsibility. However, *both* are motivated by guilt—the Caretaker stays to assuage his guilt and the Escape Artist leaves in an attempt to escape his guilt.

Anxiety and caretaking should not be mistaken for love and compassion. Although caretaking is an attempt to help someone, it's not an effective way of doing it. To alleviate their worry, Caretakers will step in and rescue or control. The confusion lies in the belief families have about their responsibility to the mentally ill person; often they assume they aren't compassionate if they *don't* worry. Nevertheless, worry is *not* compassionate, and can even get in the way of helping someone move toward recovery.

True compassion means accepting the mentally ill person but not suffering because of him or his behavior. Compassion can be understood as a detached love for another person. This means caring about someone deeply without living his life for him or attempting to make him behave in a certain way. *Compassionate responsibility results in compassionate action.* When we are acting out of a state of compassion, we do not hold feelings of anger or resentment. No matter what the outcome of the situation, we will have peace. We accept our limits and the limits of the other person. Without compassionate responsibility we will feel fear, guilt and a deprivation of confidence. Compassion allows us some perspective so that outside circumstances and the behaviors of others does not put us in a state of anxiety and panic.

As a family member, you must remember, whether or not the mentally ill person is capable of independence, no one is responsible for another's feelings, thoughts, or behavior (Stages three and five). Can you become compassionate in your love by letting go of feeling responsible and overprotective? Can you be involved with another without taking their behaviors personally? If you can't, your emotional life will remain determined by the ups and downs of your mentally ill relative or friend.

THE POWER OF YOUR THOUGHTS

Like everyone, Caretakers have feelings that fuel their behaviors. And every feeling springs from a belief or attitude. Caretakers have many feelings and beliefs that perpetuate their caretaking behavior. Emotions motivate people to caretake but it is the thought or belief behind the emotion that keeps the feeling active.

Imagine the following scene in which two friends attend a funeral:

At the funeral, they are sitting in the front row listening to the eulogy; one is sobbing profusely while the other is sitting peacefully with a look of contentment on her face. The one who is sobbing is feeling the loss of her friend intensely. She believes that the death is unjust and fate is unfair to rob such a young woman of her life. In contrast, the friend who is sitting there peacefully is remembering all the enjoyable times they spent together and is grateful for the friendship. She believes that, for whatever reason, it was time for her friend to die and, although she misses her, she accepts death as a reality for everyone. She also believes in a life after death that is a more pleasant experience than anyone can imagine.

Both women are living the same experience. However, they have different emotional responses. It is not the event that is creating the difference in their emotions but what they t*hink about* the death, their friend, and the funeral.

Listed below are beliefs and attitudes which fuel the emotions associated with caretaking. Notice how certain beliefs, e.g., "I'll do anything not to be rejected," cause you to feel a certain way. How might you change an attitude to feel better? Up till now you may have thought it was the mentally ill person or your family that caused you to feel the way you do. You may have held others responsible for how you feel. What you will discover is that regardless of the events and people around you, you can choose to feel differently by examining your beliefs and assumptions (Stage four). Review the beliefs and assumptions below to gain a better understanding of yourself and why you may feel and behave the way you do.

As a Caretaker You May Feel:

Fearful because you do not understand that there are alternatives to problems presented to you; lack faith; are skeptical about life, distrustful; have a distorted view of the world and relationships; secretly believe you are responsible for others' problems.

Guilty because you can't deal with others' disappointment; do not want to be rejected; believe saying no to someone is rejecting them; live by "musts," "shoulds," "shouldn'ts;" are dependent on approval; are manipulated or manipulative; are prone to make excuses or accept excuses from others; believe you have failed someone somehow; believe you are responsible for the troubles of those you care about.

Insecure because you are worried about the future; don't trust yourself or others; are dependent on others to make you happy; believe you will be blamed for something; believe deep down that there is something wrong with you or that you have done something wrong.

Hopeless because you believe you have lost control over your life and relationships; do not believe in a Greater Power/God; blame outside circumstances and people for your problems; believe that your past experiences dictate your future (past was difficult, future will be); believe that many things are impossible, can't be done; resist change.

Lonely because you don't trust others; hold unrealistic expectations for yourself and others; don't understand what goes into a relationship; are controlling; don't think it is wise to share your thoughts and feelings with others; won't take risks.

Angry because you do not forgive yourself or others; resent others for not meeting your expectations; resent yourself for not living up to personal expectations; try to manipulate others unsuccessfully; when others don't agree with you believe they are rejecting you; often believe that life "must" go a certain way; are prone to rationalizing your own behavior or the behavior of others.

Resentful because you are doing something you don't want to, but believe you "must"; are jealous of others; unforgiving.

Self-pitying because you take life too seriously/personally; have distorted view of life and relationships; believe that you and/or your family are being punished; believe that life is to be endured not enjoyed.

Shame because you believe you are bad, wrong, evil.

Fortunately, by recognizing the beliefs and assumptions that cause your negative feelings you can begin to give up the ones that are self-defeating and keep you stuck in the role of a Caretaker, and to replace them with attitudes that support you as a Caregiver. This commitment to change is a life-time healing process. We don't change old patterns of thought and behavior in an instant. Permanent change takes time with lots of patience and perseverance. Change is an organic process, therefore slow but enduring.

CARETAKING OR CAREGIVING

As a Caregiver you will feel free to share yourself with those whom you choose. You will begin to understand that just because others demand or expect something of you does not mean that they have a right to it and that you don't have to be in a relationship with *anyone* other than someone of your own choosing. In fact, your focus, as a Caregiver, will no longer be exclusively on the mentally ill person but on yourself and your relationship with this person and your family.

Regardless of what the problem is, the roadway to answers is understanding yourself and your relationships. Once you grasp this, you will experience an awakening—an understanding that the challenges you are facing can be handled because it is *always possible to improve oneself and how one relates to others*. For many this awakening takes place with a renewed belief in a Greater Power; a sense that happiness exists *within* oneself, or through the awareness that no one can be held hostage by someone else's life unwillingly.

In becoming a Caregiver your concept of giving changes. Providing love, care, and support becomes a matter of choices and alternatives—not ultimatums. Caregivers understand that the most you can do for another person is set an example. They learn that giving can be a joyful experience. They do not disable themselves or suffer because someone they love is mentally ill. Furthermore, when confronting difficult times, they use the power of their imaginations to guide them into myriad possibilities.

AN EXERCISE OF THE IMAGINATION

Within anyone's imagination lie solutions to the greatest of problems. The following is an exercise to help you use your imagination to open up to new possibilities for yourself and alternatives when confronting your challenges.

Imagine that you are in a different family. *Create the ideal family.* Consider being someone else in the family. If you are the parent now, be a child, if you are a spouse, be a sibling. Maybe you imagine a smaller family or a larger one. Be who you want to be, say the things you want to say to this family, and have them respond the way you dream they would. Imagine having dinner together, or sitting around in the living room. What are the conversations about and who is talking? Imagine your family taking part in a variety of activities together. Have events gone as you would like them to go. How is this family behaving? What do its members do together?

Now have someone begin getting depressed, withdrawn, or hostile. Have your ideal family handle the behavior and disruptions that accompany mental illness. Imagine everyone, including yourself, handling this challenge or crisis exactly in the way you would prefer it to be handled. What's happening? What are the conversations like now? What creative decisions are being generated within this ideal family of yours? Who is reaching out to you and who are you supporting? Take yourself and your family *through* the challenge. In time, bring the challenge or crisis to a completion. Have it end in whatever way your positive imagination generates. Now feel and imagine the family *after* the crisis. See yourself in conversation with others in your family. Enjoy the sensations and conversations that arise after the crisis.

Don't resist creating ideals. Imagining something as possible makes it more likely to come true for you. If you don't believe something is possible, how can you allow it to happen?

UNSEALING THE SPRING

Within each of us is a spring abundant with creativity, energy, love, compassion, wisdom and understanding. To unseal the spring will take a commitment to take a look within ourselves to see what is blocking the flow. When we unseal this spring within us, we can accomplish great things, overcome all obstacles.

A loyalty to someone else does not have to override a loyalty to yourself—no matter how disabled this other person may be. Caretaking must stop unless sacrificing your own peace of mind is worth temporary freedom from guilt. When you learn to care for yourself better, to stop controlling and protecting, you will find a plentiful spring of love, resources, and ideas that are your gifts to share. Remember, your most valuable resource is yourself.

4

The Escape Artists

A Choice confronts us. Shall we, as we feel our foundations shaking, withdraw in anxiety and panic? Frightened by the loss of our familiar mooring places, shall we become paralyzed and cover our inaction with apathy? If we do those things, we will have surrendered our chance to participate in the forming of the future. We will have forfeited the distinctive characteristic of human beings: namely, to influence our evolution through our own awareness.
— ROLLO MAY

As a child, living with her mother often meant fearing what she would find when she came home. As an adult she drank and took painkillers to forget her past and to deal with her loneliness. She gave herself away to the public in hopes of making up for the neglect she experienced as a child.

This briefly illustrates the tragedy of Marilyn Monroe's life, whose mother spent most of her adult life in mental institutions and whose grandmother died in one. She never knew her father and when her mother was in the hospital she lived in one foster home after another. If you are an adult child of a parent with mental illness, her story may sound familiar to you. Marilyn was an Escape Artist.

Everyone needs to escape at one time or another. Usually the frightened, angry, hurt person within us hides, unless he is quite sure it is safe to show his face. Within each member of the family torn by mental illness is an Escape Artist who keeps some feelings and concerns a secret. In addition to the Escape Artist within each family member there are those members who literally escape as a form of survival.

In contrast to the Caretaker, the Escape Artist chooses, whether consciously or not, to hide and deny his feelings, particularly during a crisis. His response to crisis is to avoid it; he feels increasingly comfortable as he removes himself from the conflict and stress around him. Instead of attempting to control a crisis by caretaking, the Escape Artist controls his environment through avoidance and isolation.

He first escapes by hiding in his room, staying away from home, abusing drugs or alcohol, or through the adrenalin high of committing petty crimes. Escape Artists want to deny that there really is a problem in the family. They are determined to cover up their feelings of anger, hurt, and abandonment.

Often, the family is unaware of the gradual withdrawal of one of its family members. Believing that the Escape Artist is adequately taking care of himself, the family generally accepts his absence; may even encourage it. Compared with the mentally ill person, the calm exterior of the Escape Artist is a blessing. When the Escape Artist succeeds at withdrawing from the family, his absence is often not noticed until years later. After all, the attention of the family is concentrated on the one apparently most in need—the mentally ill person.

As could be expected, Caretakers and Escape Artists share common attributes and experiences, such as not getting positive strokes for taking care of themselves, generally being unaware of their own feelings and needs, assuming that their problems are relatively unimportant when compared with those of others, having difficulty setting personal goals and forming mutually satisfying relationships. However, there are differences: Escape Artists are typically uninvolved in providing direct care for the mentally ill friend or relative, are unavailable during a crisis, are least likely to reach out for support or counseling, and are bystanders, in that they may see the family's problems but remain uninvolved. They become experts of isolation.

These destructive qualities are a purposeful way for these family members to survive a threatening environment.

"I haven't seen my mentally ill brother for years. I am married to a beautiful woman and we have two children. I am successful in my business as a lawyer and love my life as it is. My younger sister, Carrie, calls me during the holidays and just from the tone of her voice I know she is upset with me. I can't understand what Carrie wants me to do—come and cure my brother Sam? If she wants to stay and be all wrapped up in his life that's her business, but she doesn't have to make me feel guilty because I choose to be away from it all. My children haven't met my brother and frankly I think they can live without the experience."

Jill has an aunt who has schizophrenia. Several times a year her aunt shares Jill's room: "No one asks me if I mind sharing a room with my aunt when she visits. *But I do mind.* She spooks me. Last time she was here she told me that when she was twenty years old a dark spirit entered her brain, so now she has to read the Bible every night. She rattles on about the most frightening things and then reads the Bible aloud! If my mom didn't come in and remind her that I had school in the morning she would probably read on and on. When I try to talk to my mother she says, 'That's your aunt, she's different,' and reminds me how special these times away from the 'dorm' (that's what they call it) are for her. She visits about once every other month and during holidays. She never stays with any of the other relatives! My dad somehow gets a lot busier at the office when she stays with us. And when I can, I stay overnight at friends."

By not listening to Jill, her mother is indirectly encouraging her to find refuge elsewhere. The problem isn't so much that Jill's aunt visits—it is how the family responds to these visits. There could be approaches that would meet the needs of everyone involved. Letting the mental illness dictate the family environment is a sure way to divide the family.

Walter, now thirty-two, describes how he escaped the chaos in his home: "Looking back, I remember wandering into my home between crises. My mother always seemed to be fixing meals and drinking bourbon; my schizophrenic stepsister was either on her way to a crisis, in a crisis, or resting from one. I stayed away from home most of my high school years. At night I found a friend's house to go to and we would usually sit around and watch TV, sometimes getting high on pot. My mother and stepfather just assumed I was fine. My grades from school were fine and I never complained."

The Escape Artist feels disregarded by his family. He begins his move into hiding as he assumes that his problems are less important than the mentally ill relative's. Not wanting to be an added burden, he believes he is helping the family cope by withdrawing and becoming uninvolved. He feels safer being away from the chaos and since others in the family have become involved in caretaking there appears no need for him to do so. Indeed, the Escape Artist soon becomes emotionally isolated from the family, feeling like an outcast—a bystander. Unlike the Caretaker, who becomes more involved as the mental illness progresses, the Escape Artist becomes more and more removed.

He finds that the further he is from the mental illness the

further he is from his own fears about it. While distance may decrease his sense of responsibility, in order to escape his painful feelings, he will learn to deny there is a problem to be concerned about. He will convince himself that mental illness hasn't had any effect on him. He will deny himself his own feelings and selfworth.

DENIAL: THE GREAT ESCAPE

People have a covert survival weapon—it's called denial. Denial is a defense mechanism. "There aren't any problems in our family," "I don't drink to avoid, and I don't drink any more than anyone else," "My mother's mental illness doesn't frighten me," "He didn't commit suicide, he fell off the bridge." Denial allows us to avoid what is going on inside of us and in front of us, as this story illustrates:

> "I went to a therapist when I was about twenty-three and that decision saved my life. I'll never forget what she said about my father. *Your father has the innate ability to deny. If he doesn't want to see it—it isn't there.* He just doesn't see your mother's mental illness, for him it really isn't there.' And, although this is frustrating for me, I have come to accept that this is my father's way of coping with what must be very frightening for him to acknowledge."

Denial is a silent agreement we keep with ourselves not to think, not to ask questions, not to feel. Through it we can convince ourselves we are unaffected by the mental illness, that there are no problems within our families. The Escape Artist often witnesses the family's unsuccessful attempts to take care of the problem. Observing the frustration of others in the family, he avoids the magnitude of the problem through denial.

Not accepting the mental illness is the most obvious form of denial in these families. The Escape Artist often claims that the troubled family member is "acting crazy," or he may say the mentally ill person is "different," "odd," or "lazy," but not in need of any special treatment. Or he may create elaborate explanations for the ill person's behavior; as one brother of a schizophrenic says: "We're all crazy really, she's probably the more sane and maybe it's the rest of us who are nuts. Life is complex and we shouldn't try to change others just because they are different from us." Likewise, others discount the illness by such statements as, "He's just doing this to seek attention."

Denial is often coupled with withdrawal. In order to deny that there is a problem, an Escape Artist may withdraw.

> Margaret is frustrated by her husband, Henry, who denies that their son needs medical attention. He refuses to attend any family sessions at the mental health clinic because in his own words, "They don't know what they're talking about."
>
> "I think my husband is deathly afraid of what they will accuse him of. But he claims Don is just lazy and 'refuses to take on the adult responsibilities of life.' I know our marriage is strained. I worry that if we can't even agree on what the problem is, this marriage won't make it. I need to talk with him but he withdraws when I bring up our son Don. To get along with Henry I simply don't discuss it."

In this family the husband and other siblings escape the mother's reminders that Don has a serious problem, that they "should" take care of Don—the mother is the sole Caretaker and everyone else is an Escape Artist. Don's eldest sister is leaving to travel abroad in about two months and expresses contradictory feelings of "relief and guilt," and hopes the confusion inside will end when she is away. However, her dilemma is unlikely to be resolved simply by a trip abroad. Relationships between Caretakers and Escape Artists are strained. The Escape Artists react with guilt and anger to the requests of the Caretakers and to their reminders that they aren't doing their share. And, as the Escape Artists continue to withdraw, the Caretakers feel increasingly frustrated, angry, and abandoned:

> "My brother always excuses my father's behavior with some silly comment and then somehow finds a place to disappear to when the trouble strikes. I hate him for leaving me to pick up the pieces and then acting as if there is nothing really wrong with Dad. Sometimes I feel like the hen yelling 'the sky is falling' as my brother shrugs it off as an exaggeration. But I know the sky is falling."

> "Doesn't my sister understand, I don't *like* my ill brother and I can't stand staying around all the mess. I can't even seem to tell her that I don't want to be involved because I disagree with how they are all handling my brother's illness. We never have sat down and talked and I don't see much chance of it ever happening."

Both are trapped in the silence of their own ways of coping with the mental illness. They are both suffering, yet cast blame on the other's way of coping.

Immediate family members are not the only ones personally affected by the mental illness and denial. Relatives and friends also experience deep emotions when someone they care about is lost to mental illness or commits suicide. They, too, may learn to survive through denial.

"It Was an Accident."

> "We lived separated by only a field. Across one acre of soybeans lived my cousin Darryl, whom I loved and fought with like a brother. Living on a farm, you get used to accidents and close calls with death. I lived with the fear that one day I would come home from school to find someone buried under a broken tractor or killed by one of the many other daily hazards.

> "Then one day I did come home to find an ambulance

outside my cousin's house. Its lights were circling, sending jets of light over the field of new snow. An ache in my stomach told me my worst fear was true—that someone's life had been taken by some farm equipment that should have been discarded years ago.

"It was three days before Christmas and I was fifteen years old. I didn't dash across the field to find out what happened. In a splendid hour of comfort I sat by our Christmas tree and stared into the red and green lights. Whatever the news, I was in no rush to hear it. Some time later my older sister Karen came in. I was relieved to see my father right behind her. I wanted to run and hug him, to show my happiness that it wasn't him the ambulance came for. Instead I waited to find out who the bad news was about. My uncle? He was often so careless.

"The adults sat in the kitchen talking in low, serious tones. Quietly, I sat by the tree catching what I could of the conversation in the kitchen. I overheard my dad clearly tell my sister, 'to say it was an accident.'

"Finally I was told—my cousin Darryl was dead. I didn't expect it to be *him*, not fourteen-year-old Darryl! I asked my father, 'How did it happen?' 'By accident,' he said. 'But how?' I pressed him; he told me that Darryl had 'hung himself accidentally with a rope in the basement.' I was confused. How could someone hang himself by accident?

"There was little talk about Darryl that Christmas and the festivities seemed to pass in slow motion.

"The only comfort I felt was in playing with my sister's baby, whose cries and laughter broke through the darkness. When he cried my sister rocked him and whispered words of comfort to console him. I imagined myself crawling up in my sister's lap, hearing her soothe me, but the voice that got through to me was my own: 'No, *you* don't need to cry, you're not a baby.' "

Overlooked, in part because no one in the family discussed the death, and because there were many others who came before him who needed comfort, Karl, the man in the above story, never mourned his cousin's death. Likewise, he did not have permission to express his doubts or his fears. Later, he, too, kept the silent agreement that no one has since broken— that a fourteen-year-old boy could hang himself *accidentally* from a basement rafter eighteen feet high. Karl learned that in order to cope with stress one didn't ask questions; one denied reality and then kept quiet.

Not until he began receiving counseling about his divorce did Karl, now forty-three, understand the sorrow and anger he carried around with him about Darryl's death.

Generally, Karl is compliant in relationships: ". . . others' feelings and needs always come first. I lived in a marriage for fifteen years where I denied my own feelings." He also says: "Looking back, I blame my uncle for Darryl's death. He was a man of uncontrollable mood swings. He was either angry at everyone or preaching his favorite biblical story, the Book of Job. Our family protected him, my aunt took care of him when he couldn't work the farm, and my father would do his fields. Knowing what I know now, I would guess my uncle was mentally ill. And Darryl, well, he changed quite a bit in the year before his death, acting peculiar and hostile like his father. But for whatever reason, the world was too much for Darryl."

Karl explains that his goal now is to find out about *himself:* Karl is starting to end his denial. He is beginning to face the truth, which includes confronting his many emotions and beliefs. Karl, like any of us, cannot thrive in an environment based on denial. Denial keeps us from the truth. When you deny, you conceal your fears, evade the expectations of others, avoid decisions, make inaccurate assumptions, and flee from feelings of guilt. Through denial you continue to escape reality and it is reality you must learn to accept.

We may deny reality, because we anticipate that "accepting reality" means that we contributed to the loved one's mental illness or suicide. Too often, we falsely accuse others of wrong-doing to cover up our own sense of guilt. Believing that fault will be found in us, we may retreat into blaming others. Such accusations are typically a shield we live behind so as not to expose ourselves emotionally. Ironically, such protection becomes necessary in families in which no one is talking about his own problems and feelings. We hesitate to talk to one another for fear of what we might find—because some-times there are skeletons in the closet.

> Evelyn knows her brother has a mental illness. However, she never quite admits to herself that her mother also has serious mental health problems, proven by her frequent vis-its to the hospital. She also refuses to recognize that her father is an alcoholic. He just "drinks a lot because of the stress," she explains. She and her one sister, Shauna, are not very close and in fact haven't spoken to each other for three years. How can she admit to her mother's mental ill-ness and her father's alcoholism—who then would she have as a family?

Inevitably such denial creates a false security. Evelyn will at some point need to face the reality that her mother has a mental illness and that her father is an alcoholic. Only then can she honestly confront the effects these relationships have had on her. Otherwise, a choice to continue a lie will not only enable her father's alcoholism but will destroy her. It is in fac-ing reality that she can begin to live.

Often times denial as a way to cope with severe pain turns into forgetfulness. Most siblings and adult children in Eight Stage groups uncover other problems within the family histo-ry and relationships. These problems include neglect, emo-tional and psychological abuse, sexual abuse or dysfunction, and alcohol and drug problems. The Escape Artist therefore is often "escaping" many painful realities.

ADDICTIONS: THE DEADLY ESCAPE

Addictions shield you from your feelings and concerns. They put up a wall between you and reality and prevent you from dealing with the anger, confusion, pain, and fear you have inside you. They also prevent you from experiencing love and joy because you become numbed and unable to receive from others. Addictions can stifle your creative potential, distort your perceptions, rob you of your self-esteem, and destroy your life.

Addictions control you; soon drinking, eating, gambling, shopping, working, or another person consume more and more of your time. The addiction becomes what is most important to you. Whereas the Caretaker's primary "addiction" may be to the problems of others, Escape Artists are more likely to be addicted to drugs, alcohol, gambling, shopping, sex, or work. The Escape Artist uses an addiction to cope with his loss, deal with his guilt, ignore his feelings, and ultimately help him forget. He may drink to forget responsibility to himself and others. Ultimately, addictions generate self-neglect and an inability to meet personal needs.

Many people deny the impact of alcohol or drug *usage* as a problem. However, even occasional use of alcohol or drugs to achieve a sense of worth, to be able to face one's family, or to help express one's concerns, is a sign of a psychological dependence. Alcohol and drugs engender feelings of contentment and control; you feel good and able to handle yourself; at least until the alcohol or drug wears off. Mood-altering drugs cover up the fears of being held accountable. Alcohol and drugs are indeed a convenient way out; they give you a false sense of purpose and control as well as a means to escape and still feel as if you are in the company of others.

THE SECRET LIFE

The Escape Artist is truly living a secret life because to the outside world he often falsely appears happy, healthy, and secure. This secret life only confirms what he already knows: "The only way to survive is to remain hidden, not to let others know who you really are or how you really feel." If others found out the secret of who you really are, you worry that they wouldn't accept you—because the "real" you is a vulnerable, scared, *feeling* person. Because being emotional is believed to be a sign of weakness, not showing emotion tells others, "I'm okay, I'm in control." Escape Artists are often afraid to reveal to others their imperfections for fear of being rejected.

An Escape Artist will often seek out another person who doesn't know what he wants, doesn't talk about his feelings, and who has also disappeared into a secret world. People typically are drawn to those who support their outlook on life. Their expectations are similar: "You don't share your feelings and I won't be expected to share mine." Another common pattern is simply to avoid any intimacy with others—to isolate.

Adult children and siblings of the mentally ill often have what is called "situational" depression, anxiety, or emotional problems. Situational describes a temporary condition such as a response to environmental stress. Adult children and siblings often have lesser symptoms of their loved one's mental illness, such as anxiety, low tolerance of stress, bouts of mild depression, panic attacks and suspicion of others. Unlike the symptoms of schizophrenia or manic-depression, situational emotional disorders are usually milder and most often short-lived. Nevertheless, these emotional problems often create a great disturbance in one's life. Those who have situational depression, for example, become concerned that they too may completely break down and succumb to a mental illness, as did their relative.

Those families who encourage the open expression of feelings, talk honestly, and acknowledge everyone's needs, rather than letting the mental illness consume them, will find that situational emotional problems diminish.

Escape Artists may overcompensate for their lack of intimate relationships and feelings of guilt by seeking acceptance from others. They form relationships in which they relinquish personal power in order to be accepted, even when it means giving up themselves. They are saying, "Please notice me, please appreciate me," and will do things for others to receive this appreciation. Of course they ultimately remain Escape Artists because they are pretending to be someone they are not in order to be accepted.

It is not entirely surprising to find that some family members learn that one way to get attention is to get sick, either physically or emotionally. When someone lacks love and support, it is not unusual to seek nurturing by becoming sick. After all, it is the one in most distress who tends to get the attention. It is the squeaky wheel, the outbursts of the mentally ill, that too often get the family's nurturing. The Caretaker may become sick in order to have time out from his responsibilities and to receive some nurturing; the Escape Artist on the other hand, does it to get the attention he misses during his escapes.

SUICIDE: THE FINAL ESCAPE

It is not uncommon for some Escape Artists to consider suicide as a way out. Suicide is considered after years of personal neglect and loneliness. Suicide is a result of feeling desperate. And this desperation comes from having a limited understanding of alternative ways to deal with the problems at hand. Most people who attempt suicide are frightened. Frightened by their own lack of perspective of what they can do to take care of themselves. Furthermore, they have lost their ability to cover up their fears and feelings as a result of their addictive behaviors; the drugs, the alcohol, the adrenalin highs, or the sex are no longer escape enough. They come to believe that the only way out of their pain and confusion is to end their lives.

Wanting to end the pain is normal. To consider suicide when you are feeling desperate and alone is also normal. Most people have had thoughts of ending their life. This can be a time of acknowledging just how much suffering you are in. But there is no guarantee that your pain ends when you die. The truth is, the only way *out* is *through;* to choose to live fully, free of addictions, free from denial, free from self-destruction. Many have found it helpful to practice the following when feeling this desperate, this alone:

- **Tell yourself you have options.** There are many alternatives, you just haven't opened yourself up to them yet. Even though you may not come up with immediate alternatives keep affirming to yourself: "There are many options; I have many options of dealing with this."
- **Ask yourself : *"What in me needs to die?"*** Instead of killing yourself, ending it all, why not kill the part of you that is ready to die? What in you needs to die? Perhaps the Escape Artist, the drug addict, your sense of worthlessness, the part of you that is blind to the many possibilities that are ahead—could any of these be what needs to die?
- **Contact someone.** *Don't isolate. Don't isolate. Don't isolate.*

THE CHOICE IS YOURS: ESCAPING OR LIVING?

The way in which we live our lives and interact with others is developed through our family relationships as we grow up. Escape Artists are not taught how valuable it is to get their own needs met in relationships. Not all forms of escape are as life-threatening as drug usage. In fact, withdrawal from the family protected them from the disruption at home, enabling them to survive. The issue is not so much that Escape Artists made wrong choices—it is whether or not they need to continue making the same choices. They should not assume that "This is how things are for me." It is the belief that they have to continue escaping, hiding, or avoiding in order to survive that keeps them stuck in destructive patterns.

Relationships are the soil for personal development. For

Escape Artists, it is going to take getting involved with their own lives and the lives of others for them to start living fully. There are several ways to work on evolving into a healthy person, to experience mutually supportive relationships, to get beyond just coping with life. The choice is between escaping life or living life; being part of life or being absent from life. Reality has some pain, some challenges, and it also holds an abundance of joy, creativity, and love. Up until now, being an Escape Artist may have brought them some security, some distance between them and what troubled them, but it also brought them loneliness and low self-esteem.

There is no magic cure for becoming healthy. They will never be rescued from their troubles. And they cannot afford to wait to be rescued. To remain Escape Artists or Caretakers will lead them to absolute self-neglect. Their lives will not be their own. They must help themselves. They will soon discover that as they change and take risks, their fears and doubts will shrink in the shadow of their growth.

Change will sooner or later mean breaking the silent agreements that keep them Escape Artists, Pleasers, Victims, or Codependents. Because of the silent agreements made in their families, they must be prepared to challenge family patterns.

The past is available to learn from, not to live in, and the future is there to prepare for, not to fear. We can unlearn the harmful effects of the past. We can overcome our addictions. We can find intimacy and love in every relationship we choose. The choices we make *today* will determine our present and our future.

Until recently Tanya's choice was to escape: "Not until I was forced to slow down and take a look did I realize why I was so unhappy, so unproductive. I experienced depression myself for ten years. I have even considered suicide. But I couldn't kill myself and leave my parents alone with the responsibility for my mentally ill sister. It didn't even cross my mind that they might miss me, or that there were other alternatives. At that time the only thing that kept me alive was not wanting to burden my parents. I never guessed answers would be found just by taking the time to take care of *myself*. To ask myself what I needed. I was too afraid to look into myself. I was afraid I wouldn't find a way out, that again I would be faced with the terrible fear that there are no answers—that there is no sanity in this world. Now I am beginning to understand that even the worst experience is something I can overcome—*that I can walk away from somebody else's crisis without making it my own!* I look at the world differently now, and what's happened is that it is an entirely new place, a much more inviting place; I have no desire to think of a way out."

Every human being is a precious resource unto himself. A resource that deserves the finest love and attention by its owner. If your choices of escape have kept you from truly being alive, it is time for you to choose life. Listed below are some ideas on how to start.

- Be open to alternative ways of handling the problems in your life.
- Seek an open-mindedness that allows you to gain a wider perspective of your life and relationships—don't assume you have all the answers from your present viewpoint.
- If you use alcohol or drugs, stop using them altogether and observe what happens.
- Join a therapy or self-help group (Eight Stages for example).
- If you are an alcoholic, or engage in any of the various addictions, join an appropriate support group to assist you in giving up your addiction.
- Identify one creative project or goal you have been putting off and start it today.
- Stop seeking approval from others; begin to focus on what *you* want and need.
- Work on the Eight Stages. (Refer to Chapter Eight.)

- Seek professional counseling/spiritual guidance.
- Begin to share your feelings and thoughts with others whom you would like to trust.
- Read material on personal growth and family relationships, and/or attend seminars and workshops geared toward personal growth and healing family relationships.

Emerging as a healthy, *alive* person is not free of risks but it is worth the effort it takes. In reality there are many avenues to receiving love, support, and expressing creative energy. Through the dispelling of secrets and understanding how destructive patterns developed within the family, it becomes possible for family members to take the steps to come alive, to come out of hiding, and to greet the world around them.

A Dive Into Non-escapism

The surest way to undo the variety of ways you escape is to arrive fully into your life—*whatever* that includes. One of the surest ways to arrive is through the practice of Mindfulness (awareness) meditation. Mindfulness brings you into the moment, the present experience, whatever it may be. It gives you the ability to focus your thoughts, live fully in the present, follow through on your goals and accept the circumstances of your life in a conscious and balanced manner. Chapter Six offers a brief introduction to mindfulness meditation, along with recommended reading to further your practice. Remember, it takes a lot more energy to escape than it does to live your life honestly.

5

A Delicate Balance

It is not because things are difficult that we do not dare; it is because we do not dare that they are difficult.

— SENECA

We can never discover new oceans unless we have courage to lose sight of the shore.

— ANDRÉ GIDE

"Although we did not live together, my life and my brother's were inextricably linked. I tried numerous ways to get along with him, to help him, or make him help himself. I would attempt to coerce my parents into trying the many treatments I thought would cure him. Inevitably, I ended up feeling angry with my whole family and then feeling guilty because of my anger. Finally, I realized it wasn't *him* I was angry with but the *illness*. I can now say, without guilt, that I hate the illness—what it has done to me, my family, and my brother. Most of the time now I can separate my brother from his mental illness. I have begun to understand that the illness doesn't have to consume every part of our lives. This separation has finally brought some peace and balance into my life."

The woman in the above story has created a separation between herself and her brother's problems, but not through escape; it is an *internal* separation and it allows her to remain involved with her brother without getting caught up in trying to rescue or caretake.

Separating yourself from another's problems does not mean you are rejecting him or are unwilling to help him. Rather, you are no longer taking on the responsibility for his life. Separating yourself from others in this manner gives you permission to take care of yourself *first*. In fact, you must take care of yourself before you are truly able to give to others. An internal separation allows you to take care of yourself *in a way that does not interfere with others getting their own needs met*. You use your initiative and personal resources to improve the quality of your life, at the same time positively affecting those around you.

In order to create a delicate balance in our lives, each of us must tend not only to our physical needs but also to our emotional, psychological, spiritual, and interpersonal needs. Because of the demands of the mentally ill person, your needs may have been set aside or postponed. But take a closer look at all your relationships. You may find yourself in friendships, in a job, and in a marriage where you are providing far more than you are receiving. Are you able to be honest with these people about what you want and need? Are you experiencing intimacy within these relationships? If you aren't, stop the charade that these relationships are adequate, when they are not. Start to recognize that there can be more for you in all your relationships and that you can do something to improve them. However, in order to create a balance in your life, you must stop pretending that a life *out* of balance is satisfactory.

THE DEMISE OF THE PRETENDER

Everyone pretends at one time or another. We may pretend that we enjoy something we actually dislike because being honest provokes feelings of discomfort. Sometimes pretending involves convincing ourselves and others that we are something we are not. It may mean showing how brave we are, when in fact we are scared, or not showing that we are hurt when someone says he doesn't love us. We may pretend in order to protect ourselves from expected ridicule and embarrassment. When we pretend we conceal our feelings behind a facade of calm and indifference.

Many people pretend to live up to the expectations of others. As shown earlier, Pleasers behave the way they assume others want them to in order to feel appreciated. Pleasers are great pretenders. Adult children and siblings of the mentally ill often pretend they don't mind that their needs come second, or that it doesn't matter if the family overlooks their accomplishments while taking care of the mentally ill person. Most harmful, however, is pretending that you are feeling well when you are not, that you are happy when you feel hurt inside, that you don't need others to comfort you when of course you do.

There are many dangers to living a lie; you may forget how to show your feelings, how to be open and honest. Without openness, honesty, and the ability to ask for what you need, you cannot experience true intimacy with anyone. In fact, pretending rules out honesty and openness. It makes it impossible to get what you need—because you are either pretending you don't need anything, or that you need "x" when what you really need is "y." You are then disappointed when you end up with "nothing" or "x."

On Becoming a Caregiver

As you become more honest with yourself and others, you become more aware that someone else's behavior doesn't cause you to be unhappy—it is *your* response to his behavior that causes your unhappiness. Too often, relatives of the mentally ill feel responsible for others and comforted by others' approval. "Happiness" becomes dependent on what others do or do not do, and family members live on the successes and failures of the mentally ill person, much like people who live in grass huts whose lives depend on the predictability of the weather. If the weather is stormy and floods prevail, their lives are tragic. If the weather is pleasant, they remain in the grass huts, enjoying the temporary calm.

The truth is that all peace and strength come from a place within yourself. Nothing anyone else does or fails to do can take away your inner happiness unless you allow it. In fact, it is this inner strength that can keep you from losing your peace of mind during a crisis or conflict. Through the process of becoming a Caregiver, you realize that all your feelings—anger, happiness, guilt, calm, joy, and fear—come from a place *within* yourself. Your feelings are an indication of what you believe about yourself and others but are not dictated by outside circumstances. Just as you cannot help anyone without his consent, no one can make you unhappy without your consent. Don't consent to feeling unhappy. Don't consent to neglecting yourself.

When the outside world is destructive or chaotic, the *only* place to find peace is within. But to find this peace you must be willing to search your inner reservoir of resources and strength. In hundreds of stories about survivors of the Nazi death camps we are told how their belief that there was life beyond the camp's fence kept them alive. Their hope of being reunited with family and their knowledge that others were fighting to free them helped them survive. Those who have inner strength and hope can survive any tragedy. They can learn to see beyond the adversity that surrounds them in the same way that you can learn that there is life beyond the fence which mental illness places around you and your family.

Carolyn's whole life consisted of working and taking care of her mother: "My mother has been diagnosed with schizophrenia, borderline personality disorder, and compulsive behaviors; the diagnoses are as numerous as the doctors she chooses. To me she has always been an angry, manipulative, lonely woman. Yet, I couldn't pull myself away from her. Eating seemed to be my only defense against my own loneliness. At thirty-one I weighed two hundred and ten pounds. Finally, someone at work suggested Overeaters Anonymous. I thought, if I didn't get out and get help I would live my life fat and lonely. I realized at my first OA meeting that my problems were much more than being overweight. This may sound strange, but I had never really asked myself, 'Am I happy with my life?' With the support of my group I stopped pretending I was satisfied with myself. I could have died of obesity in my attempt to continue covering up my unhappiness."

In this story, Carolyn, at the age of thirty-one, still lived with her mentally ill mother. Every time she discussed living on her own, her mother would do something to sabotage Carolyn's decision to move, such as becoming depressed or threatening to cut off any contact. Not until Carolyn attended Overeaters Anonymous did she understand the motivation behind her eating habits. Carolyn ate to insulate herself from her manipulative mother and to cover up her pain and boredom. Finally, after three years of Overeaters Anonymous and counseling, Carolyn moved out of her mother's house. Her mother now refuses to have any contact with Carolyn but continues to live successfully on her own. During the same time, Carolyn lost fifty-two pounds, maintained her weight loss, and became actively involved with friends from her support group.

A GREATER POWER

When family members believe that the mental illness is stronger than anything they have within themselves, when they believe that mental illness is proof that there is no Greater Power or fairness in the world, they are in great danger. Without belief in a Greater Power, without perspective, pessimism settles in and permeates every aspect of life. A Greater Power can be anything you believe is more powerful than the adversity in the world. It is a source of spiritual strength, it is greater than the mental illness, greater than your negative thoughts, greater than your pain. For some, a Greater Power is viewed as "God." This is not the only source that can be viewed as a Greater Power. It can be a benevolent energy, the Buddha, a power within yourself, a philosophy or healing process, religious practices, or nature. The choice is yours.

Giving up a belief in a Greater Power, as well as faith in the community, trust in the support of others, or hope for positive outcomes are often consequences of living with a disabled or dis-eased person. It's hard for families to hold onto any hope as they witness someone they love become disabled by mental illness. Personal faith in God or in a Greater Power becomes increasingly difficult to maintain as prayers appear to remain unanswered. As the mother of a schizophrenic son says angrily, "I get to the part in 'The Lord's Prayer' that says, 'thy will be done,' and I think 'No! Not if *this* is his will.' *Why* I ask, does God permit such a horrible thing to happen to someone?"

Fortunately, faith in a Greater Power can be reclaimed. When you go in search of your spiritual strength, remember *that which you are searching for is also searching for you.* Start by talking with others who are leading more balanced lives. Because they put their needs first, these people are more likely to be genuine in expressing their feelings and involved with people who also live balanced lifestyles. You can learn from others. Discover what others think, feel, and do to experience gratifying lives. This may rekindle confidence and strength within yourself. This is why so many people benefit from hearing success stories of those who live with similar challenges. Alcoholics Anonymous uses this approach in its groups when someone shares a story of recovery. It is not the tragedies that others listen for but how the person remains on the path of recovery. This is the value of Stage One, where you share your story, your life history with others in a group. The best people to go to are those who have dealt effectively with similar problems and experiences.

Like Donna, many attend their first family self-help group unsure of what to expect and fearful of expecting too much: Donna sat down outside the circle even though chairs were available inside it. Her arms were crossed against her chest and on her lap sat a large black purse which covered most of her small frame. She looked up and smiled when we greeted her, but she quickly looked back to the floor with her face returning to a frown. No one has to talk in the group, but all are invited to share their experiences and ask for advice if they want it. Donna introduced herself quickly, talking in brief sentences and a sharp tone. "I came because my counselor suggested it. My stepmother is a recovering alcoholic and my stepsister is labeled 'schizophrenic.' Whatever that means. Doctors don't know everything. I can't understand why my father married my stepmother. Maybe I shouldn't be here. I don't think there is a group for someone with these problems. Is there? This group is only if you have a family member with chronic mental illness. And besides, my coming to such groups won't change anything in my family. Has it changed anything for any of you? The mentally ill person is still mentally ill, right?"

A sure sign of hopelessness is believing there is no place for you—no group, no person who understands or can help you. In the above story, Donna is asking for reassurance that, yes, this group is the place for her. She needs to hear the stories of others in the group who are also dealing with more than the problems of mental illness in a family member. She needs to understand that she is not alone, that there are many solutions that she can live with, that there is a power greater than the mental illness. For many this power is demonstrated through the compassion and strength received from others.

To begin rekindling your faith, attend a group which offers the Eight Stage Healing Process or help get a group started in your area. For more on this, Chapter 9 offers guidance on how you can start and facilitate your own Eight Stage self-help group. Talk to others and look for the thread of healing that binds you together:

> "I had a sister who committed suicide several years ago. I lost faith in anything after my sister killed herself by jumping off a bridge only three blocks from my apartment. Nothing made any sense. I was finishing graduate school in counseling and thought, 'Hey I'm the one who needs help!' A year ago I came across a group that was set up to help siblings and adult children of the mentally ill. We worked the Eight Stage Healing Process together which helped me understand that life doesn't have to be a constant battle. Even though I also have a younger brother in the hospital with schizophrenia and am not sure what his or my future holds, I know I can make it—that I can be a good counselor, and enjoy my life because that's what I choose.
>
> "At the last group I attended, a new participant asked me what the difference was between her and me. She commented that I seemed to have my life 'all together.' I wanted to cry with joy; she was right, I am more 'together' now. I replied by telling her that the difference between us is that I believe life will continue to get better for me, that I have faith, and that I don't have to be in pain because others around me are in pain. The difference is she's working on Stage One—Awareness, and I am now working on Stage Eight—Growth. I'm not sure she understood. I hope she

comes back to find out for herself."

THE ART OF A BALANCED LIFE

Life can be balancing act. When your attention is more on others than on yourself, when you are abusing alcohol or mood-altering drugs, when your needs are not being met, your life is out of balance. Life can be like walking a tight rope. If your attention is not focused on yourself, on your feet on the rope, you can be too distracted by the audience and you will surely fall. Living in balance will always mean taking care of yourself, making sure your attention is focused on your needs and your life, focused on your beliefs and actions. A balanced life is therefore a *focused* life.

The only way for you to bring about positive change in your life is to *be willing to do things differently*. You will need to learn the skills of balancing on a tight rope, of focusing your attention on yourself while still being involved with others. This chapter suggests four ways to be involved in a variety of relationships and still maintain serenity and independence. These four suggestions are designed to assist you further in becoming a Caregiver:

1. Identify and Ask for What You Need.

Everyone needs food and water. Obviously a lack of food or water will result in death more quickly than a lack of love. However, without connectedness to others, without psychological security, and without spiritual support, a person's life is also endangered.

- Adult Children and Siblings of the mentally ill need recognition and validation of their feelings and experiences.
- Spouses of the mentally ill need emotional support from others to deal with the conflicts they face.

- Parents need guidance and support in helping their family live effectively with the mental illness.
- The mentally ill need adequate treatment and acceptance from the community.
- Children of mentally ill parents need nurturing and love.
- All family members need to have faith that there is something more powerful than the mental illness.

If these needs are not met, a person's life will degenerate.

Stephanie was an expert at caring for her mentally ill mother and younger sister but she was not prepared when it came time to take care of herself: During her first three years as a teenager, Stephanie's home life was stressful and chaotic. She once came home from school to find her mother had overdosed on medications. Many times, Stephanie considered suicide herself, yet she didn't want to be like her mother. Later, when she was old enough to move out, her younger sister became violently ill with pneumonia. Not trusting that her mother could adequately care for her younger sister, Stephanie remained at home. Three years later she finally moved out, only to find herself isolated, afraid, and insecure. She was accustomed to taking care of others but not herself. She soon became depressed. "Am I mentally ill too?" she sometimes wondered. "Why can't I seem to make things work out for me?" She shared her concerns with an aunt and when she was asked, "What is it that would help you, Stephanie?" she didn't have an answer. She just knew what she *didn't* want—she didn't want to return home, she didn't want to be depressed, and she didn't want to feel so alone.

Stephanie never thought to ask herself, "What do *I* need?" Once you realize that you too have ignored some of your own needs, you may mourn lost opportunities. You may regret not having taken better care of yourself. "I have been floundering for a long time. I'm thirty-four years old and I haven't finished college. I'm not sure what I want to do with the rest of my life—I'm only sure of the many things I *don't* want for myself," confided the son of a mentally ill mother. As in the above examples, most people are more aware of the trouble areas in their lives and what they don't want. When you are unhappy with something in your life, it is easy to point at it and say, "I don't like this," or "I wish that would change."

Try This Exercise

Think about the last time you were unhappy or dissatisfied. What were you unhappy about in this situation? What were the events and who was involved? How were others behaving? How were the actions of others causing you to feel? Did something you like break? Did your mentally ill relative or friend behave in a way that upset you? Were you disappointed with someone or afraid of what might happen?

At the time of the incident, were you more aware of your unhappiness and what you weren't getting than you were about how you could improve the situation? Did your actions and feelings reflect your dissatisfaction or were you trying to communicate to others what you wanted?

At the time of the incident, were you aware of possible solutions to the problem? Can you now identify what you wanted or *needed* in that situation?

Chances are you were more preoccupied with your sadness or concern over your disappointment or loss than with creating alternatives—*your attention was focused on the problem*. This is true for most people.

If you cannot come up with a list of what you need in a certain situation or relationship, start with what you *don't* need, with what bothers you, in order to find out what you *do* need. Try this next exercise for practice in discovering what you need. Take the time to write a list of at least three things you *don't* need or a list of three problem areas in your life. Take a look at the list written by Stephanie:

I'm afraid I'm going to be like my mother.
I don't want to fail at living on my own.
I feel depressed and frightened.

With each statement Stephanie is actually revealing what she needs and what she wants her life to be like. The following are examples of Stephanie changing her "don't needs" and problem areas to "needs" and options:

I need to be capable of taking care of myself and to be more
    in control of my emotions and life.
I want to be independent.
I need to feel happy about myself.

Take ten minutes now and write out your list of three things you don't need or three problem areas in your life. Then write out their reverse, as in the above example. After this exercise you may find that you have a more definite idea of what you need. However, confusion or doubt may set in when you consider *how* you are going to meet those needs. You may even feel scared and guilty about these needs of yours. But don't let these feelings stop you, keep going.

Get Specific

Next, get specific about what you need from yourself and others. The vaguer you are about what you need, the less likely you are to get it. To get specific, take one of your needs and write it down on a piece of paper. Here Stephanie's list will be used as further illustration. She stated: "I need to feel happy about myself." From this statement it is difficult to know exactly what will make her happy. Her answers to the three following questions will lead to a clearer understanding of what she needs.

1. *How* will you know when your need is met? What will and

won't be happening? Describe it. In Stephanie's case she will describe what "happiness" will be like for her.

2. *Who* **else besides yourself has to be involved?** Who can support or assist you in getting your need met? Who will be involved in Stephanie's image of happiness?

3. *When* **is this need going to be met?** What is your timetable? How long can Stephanie go on being unhappy? When will she begin to create this image of happiness for herself?

The more concrete you are in describing your need the more likely you are to satisfy it. Stephanie's answers to the above questions follow. You can do this with the one need you chose to write at the top of your page. Those comments that are specific are underlined.

1. I will know I am happy when I am <u>living on my own for a while without feeling scared.</u> Happiness will feel safe. Happiness will mean I trust myself more and I am <u>involved with my work and friends.</u> I will have at least <u>one social plan a week.</u> Mostly, I will <u>feel less anxious.</u>

2. I will <u>have at least one friend</u> with whom I do fun things and with whom I can talk. I can see myself <u>involved in dance</u> or maybe <u>working out with someone at the YWCA.</u> I will be <u>less involved with my family.</u> Ideally, they will encourage me to be more independent and find other ways to get help besides calling on me. <u>I will be able to say no to them when I have other plans. I will have other plans</u> so I can say no, and these plans will involve other people. I will <u>get involved in an Eight Stage group,</u> and to help me deal with my anxiety I will <u>seek the help of a therapist.</u>

3. This need is going to be met as soon as I enroll in a class and work on making friends. I will have to join a class or the YWCA. I can make a point of getting to know somebody I work with. I could even consider taking a class to improve my job skills and meet others. <u>I'll start this Monday by asking a coworker out to lunch and looking for a class through the local college. I will be involved in a support group by the end</u>

<u>of this month and start seeking professional help in two weeks.</u> I have written all this down on my personal calendar.

Once you have taken all your needs and made them more specific it is time to ask for them. Getting your needs met will involve others whom you have chosen to help and encourage you. Even in the example of meeting one's spiritual needs, attending a church, synagogue or sangha is the social context by which this need may be met. As shown in the above case, Stephanie will make her needs known to the following people: her family—to ask that they make fewer demands on her; her acquaintances—to demonstrate her desire to get to know them better; her coworkers—to express an interest in socializing; a counselor and an Eight Stage group—to help her deal with family and personal problems. Involving others requires taking risks and extending trust. Risk comes with asking others for support and trust comes from letting go and allowing others to comfort you.

If Not Now, When?

Success in meeting your needs comes with following through on your plans. When you *do* something, when you take action, you will get results. Taking such action in meeting your own needs unseals the inner spring of creativity and self-worth. When you begin, don't worry about the outcome or how others will respond—act and be open to what happens. Using the exercise just described will help you develop the skills to get what you need and explore many avenues in order to meet those needs. Stage Eight: Goal Setting, will help you further with this. Don't put it off any longer. Take risks. Value yourself enough to risk change, risk asking of yourself and others what you need, *what you deserve,* in order to live fully.

2. Develop a Network of Support *Outside* the Family.

Social isolation is certainly not a problem unique to families of the mentally ill. A surprising number of people lack friendships and connection to a community. Most people's primary support comes from their families. Both Caretakers and Escape Artists have trouble developing a support network outside the family; the Caretaker's relationships are almost exclusively with family members, while the Escape Artist is often without any support system at all. This lack of a support network adds to the stress on these individuals. No one can heal in isolation; we all need strong friendships and connections to a community.

It doesn't matter whether you are the spouse, parent, sibling, or adult child of a mentally ill person, it is essential that you get support from outside the family. Furthermore, you will discover that many of your needs will be better met by those other than your immediate family.

Anna's grandmother committed suicide when Anna was fourteen. But Anna's mother never opened up about her past. She didn't share her feelings. Instead, she behaved as though emotions were too personal to disclose to others: "I never learned to trust myself, to believe in myself, because no one around me believed in me. I was so full of anger and fear that I could only find refuge in work. I didn't have one close friend, only acquaintances from work. I finally went to a counselor just to have someone listen to me. During my first session, she detailed my behaviors which led her to the conclusion that I came from a family where either one or both parents were alcoholic. All the symptoms she described fit me to a T—the fear of intimacy, the distrust of myself and others, the self-deprecation, and the isolation. But neither of my parents was an alcoholic; in fact they opposed the use of alcohol. My father was quite strict and overprotective. I asked my therapist if having a grandmother who committed suicide and a brother who is mildly retarded and mentally ill could cause me to feel and behave the way I do. Her reply made me both sad and relieved: 'Your parents' inability to be honest with you about the family's problems, their withholding of affection, and their overzealous and inconsistent discipline of you and your brother, are behaviors similar to that in families with alcoholism. Your family environment made it difficult for you to form relationships, take risks, make decisions, or trust yourself and others.' After I heard this I felt angry at my parents, yet relieved—now I understood my distrust of others and why it was so difficult for me to be in relationships."

Anna can always choose to break the coping patterns passed on to her and replace them with alternative ones. She can begin reaching out to others. It will feel uncomfortable and frightening at times, but through relationships outside the family, she can find encouragement and support.

A support network outside the family prevents you from being engulfed by the family's problems and silent agreements. Those outside the family are less likely to accept your family's silent agreements without question, thus allowing you to gain some perspective. Once you start expanding your support network, you will experience a shift in family relationships, especially if they have been a primary avenue of support for you. Each family member will choose to respond to the growth in you in his own way. It is crucial that you develop a support network outside the family in order to have others who help you through your transformation. You deserve others who will be there just for you. You need to be part of a community that supports your trying new styles of living.

These people in your support network can be your shoulder to lean on, your cheering section, or those with whom you relax and play. The ideal social network for family members of the mentally ill would include the following:

- A therapy or self-help group of others who are dealing successfully with similar problems.
- At least two friends who can empathize but do not necessarily have a mentally ill relative themselves.
- A trusting relationship with a professional counselor.

- Friends who do not depend on drinking and mood-altering drugs for entertainment. This does not mean total sobriety if alcohol is not a problem for you, but rather a sensitivity to the effects of such substances.
- A time of recreation with others at least once a week. This time is important and should not be neglected because of the needs or problems of others.
- A group or organization which emphasizes spiritual growth. This can be a church, synagogue, sangha, yoga class, meditation center, ritual or prayer group.
- Involvement in some activity, group, or organization that caters to your personal interests. This could mean a volunteer job or adult education class.

Now, compare your present lifestyle with the ideal described above. The farther you are away from it, the more your life is out of balance. You may want to use the above model to begin creating your own support network. When you decide to develop one for yourself, remember to let others within your network know what you need. Furthermore, be confident that there are others also in search of friendship and support.

3. Learn to Say No.

Why learn to say no? In the spirit of a balanced life, saying no is both healthy and necessary. Learning to say no will increase the opportunities for getting your needs met. But, no is a strong word, often communicating rejection, refusal, or anger. However, no is also a word signifying independence and self-protection.

Many people can say no to others only by becoming emotionally or physically ill. The illness provides an excuse for them to refuse others' requests. Sometimes they are pushed to the point of ill health because of the physical and mental stress of always trying to please others. Getting sick as a reaction to stress is destructive. Other destructive ways to say no include avoidance, violence, procrastination, perfectionism, drug or alcohol use, lying, and manipulation. Such methods of saying no can easily become a pattern because these are the means through which we gain relief from expectations and obligations. Ironically, these obligations are often self-imposed.

If you are ill, emotionally or physically, others will typically expect less of you and, consequently, you may avoid making difficult decisions.

A twenty-nine-year-old woman tells this story about herself: "First I used cocaine to handle the stress of dealing with my brother Eric's illness. I used it to help me cope with all the problems that I was constantly confronted with. Later, it helped distract me. I could remain detached from my family's problems when I was high on booze and cocaine. During that time everything was all right and I felt in control. I could manipulate others when I was high. When my parents call me (which is often because I am the only other child), it usually has to do with my brother. And how can I refuse them help? Why is it so hard to tell my parents I disagree or that I won't do things their way—that I have another way of doing things? I finally stopped taking cocaine because it began to destroy me. Now I am battling my own depression. One saving grace about my depression is that my parents expect less of me and I can rest."

Amanda, the woman in the above story, is in danger of relying on her depression as the only way to refuse her parents' requests because it permits her to withdraw from them and free herself from their expectations of her. However, less self-defeating ways of saying no and setting limits are also available to Amanda.

Your Right to Refuse

If you are one of many who finds yourself saying yes to

requests when you would prefer to say no, it is time to learn to say *no*.

When you begin to say no to your family's coping strategies, they may respond with confusion or anger. Most likely, they do not have the intention of hurting or manipulating you. They are simply taking care of the one they feel is in most need—the mentally ill person.When Amanda in the above example says no, by disagreeing or by refusing her parents' requests, their relationship will be at odds. Until now, going along with her parents kept peace in the family. When Amanda says, "I disagree and I want you to consider other possibilities because this involves me," the family will be in conflict, particularly if each member of the family has a different idea of how best to resolve the problem. Keep in mind, however, that each idea is a possible solution. Avoiding conflict within your family is nonproductive. Disagreement, although uncomfortable, most often leads to solutions.

When you change you no longer are predictable and interactions may, temporarily, become uncomfortable. People fear that when others change they too will be expected to do things differently. They relied on you to behave a certain way and now you are telling them, "No, I want things done differently, I am a different person." They may even prefer you as you were and find it hard to understand the reasons you choose to change. Don't be surprised if the new you isn't received warmly; this only confirms the need for a support network that encourages and validates the new you—the person who can and does say no.

Practice Saying No

To understand the process and power of saying no, think of a recent situation in which someone asked you for something. Say, for example, that someone has asked you to come home for an uncle's birthday celebration and to pick up your mentally ill cousin from the state hospital on your way. You don't want to attend because you don't expect to enjoy yourself and you have other plans. However, there are family members who are expecting you to attend. You are having difficulty deciding on whether to respond: "Yes, I will go," or "No, I have other plans." Practice choosing by imagining what a yes or a no would be like in this case. Describe the consequences if your answer were yes; then describe the consequences of a refusal, of your saying no. Include in your comparison what is expected of you in both situations. For example, what is expected of you if you say yes? Ask yourself if you are freely meeting others' expectations or somehow feel coerced. Does refusing this request mean you could be doing something else instead?

After you have described the results of both yes and no responses, decide which outcome meets your needs best. Ultimately, you will have to practice this in real life, in your real relationships. Get comfortable with refusing others' requests and discover the independence and protection in the word no.

Part of the power to say no comes with the ability to say, "I will get back to you about that after I think about it some more." Don't let yourself be pressured into a quick response, because it is more likely that you will be manipulated into doing something you might otherwise choose not to. Give yourself the time to decide freely what is best for you. If it is difficult for you to feel peaceful about a decision, let it go for a while. Perhaps it is too soon for you to decide. When you say yes to a request it should be because you have thought it through and believe it is in your best interest as well as theirs. For more on this, Chapter 6 goes into detail on decision making and creative problem-solving.

4. In All Circumstances, Be True To Yourself.

Being true to yourself means having the ability to maintain your integrity even in the midst of chaos and controversy, to be genuinely involved with others while not taking on their perceptions and reactions to circumstances. To be true to yourself, you must value yourself, imperfections and all.

Mental illness creates many subtle pressures on family members that affect them deeply but are not necessarily obvious to them. The demand made on family members to yield their integrity to others in the family is one such pressure. Any time you act against your own judgment, are manipulated or shamed into doing something, or let others make important decisions for you, you are relinquishing your integrity. There is virtually no situation in which you *have* to give up yourself, your truth. For example, even when you are given instructions by an employer, you can still exercise integrity by choosing how to respond.

Julie describes how her life changed when she finally stopped living in the fear that others would discover she was just a fake: "My life was ideal. I was married to a man who loved me. I had been working at a job I cared about for five years, and I had recently been promoted. I had friends and my life had meaning. Yet, something was out of sync in my life. I felt stifled at my job but no freer on my time off. Finally, I decided to leave for another job which promised more money and responsibilities. What happened next was a turning point in my life. My supervisor at work came into my office three days before I left. I was sifting through papers and books, deciding what to take with me. He told me the director had asked him to add a report to my personnel file that stated the mistakes I had made on the job. My biggest fear had come true: others had discovered that I wasn't perfect after all, in fact I was a failure—a fake. That evening my fantasies and fears kept me awake. I worried about how I had to *prove* to everyone that I was all right, that I loved my job, cared about my clients, and that I did my best to make the program a success. But who would believe me, a failure—a fake?"

Julie was faced with a time in her life when she could easily relinquish her integrity, which would mean giving up everything to prove to others she was an okay person. Or, she could take this situation as an opportunity to learn that no one could take her integrity, *it was something she had to give away*. But what does this story have to do with families of the mentally ill? Through this experience, Julie realized how she first learned to forfeit her personal truth.

When she was twelve her older brother began to show signs of schizophrenia. He soon withdrew from school because he was paranoid and heard voices. He lost contact with most of his friends. He sat at home consumed by his fear and anger as Julie finished school and made friends. When Julie would come home at night her brother would tease her relentlessly, telling her that she "wasn't all that great and he knew how stupid and sick she *really* was." He claimed he could read her mind and it seemed to her he sometimes could. He knew her insecurities and held this power over her throughout their adolescence. Now, through her more recent experience, she realized that she carried around with her this dark side, this fear that someday she would be discovered—that she was a failure.

"I had to save myself from my own fears and self-doubt. I decided then that the director's perception of me was faulty. I began to believe in myself and didn't let her report cause me to doubt myself. I knew that the best thing for me was to let her put whatever she wanted into my personnel file; that I still knew I was a good person, talented and smart. I realized that my brother's teasing and hostility were because he disliked *himself* so much that he was ashamed of himself. *His hostility was only a sign of his pain, not my worth.* And the director's report was a sign of *her* perceptions and her reaction to my decision to leave, not my worth. Nothing ever came of the report, and I am successful and appreciated in my new job. I will never give myself away again by fearing that people will discover that I am a failure."

It may be that you too have grown accustomed to giving up your "self," your integrity. Caretaking, ignoring your own needs, or believing other people's negative assumptions are all ways of relinquishing your "self" to others. Perhaps someone has said to you, "You are not a very good person," or "You've made some terrible mistakes." You may have chosen to go out of your way to prove him wrong, or you may have felt handicapped by what he said. By responding in either of these ways, you have given away your personal power. Such judgmental comments are made out of anger, distrust, hurt, or jealousy.

When someone expresses anger, distrust, or jealousy toward you, this tells you something about *that person*—it doesn't necessarily say anything about you. You can also be compassionate towards other's negative emotions and actions, knowing we all get caught in them at some time or another. But there is no reason to take on such negative comments. When your mentally ill loved one strikes out at you with a comment like, "You're selfish and don't really care about me," is your response to prove him wrong? If so, you are taking his comment personally. Hurtful comments usually come from people who are feeling hurt inside. Also, the mentally ill person may lack the skills to express his feelings appropriately.

Furthermore, a person who truly cares about you won't tell you that you are worthless or constantly remind you of your faults; he won't deal with you indirectly by filing reports or sending others to deliver his bad news. Someone who cares about you will talk to you in a direct and supportive manner, and his conversation will be free of blame and judgmental comments.

You can keep your integrity by not reacting impulsively to others' judgmental comments about you. When others are unwilling or unable to deal with you directly and honestly, refuse to remain involved with them. You can choose to tell them how you feel about their comments, but don't wait around for them to change or go out of your way to "prove them wrong." It is not in your power to change other people's minds. Keeping your integrity means that you are responsible for your own feelings and attitudes and hold others accountable for theirs.

TAKE RISKS AND MOVE ON

At this point you may be thinking, "I take risks! I have lived from one risk to another!" But you may be confusing risk-taking with being accustomed to crisis.

Gilda tells this story of her reaction to a crisis: "I was at a local cafe with some friends. I went up to the counter to pay my bill and noticed the cashier was pale. A man was robbing the place and to frighten me he put the gun to my side. I felt nothing. My only thought was to pay my bill, which I did. The thief proceeded to take money from the cash register as I returned to my table. Then when I sat down I felt a twinge of fear. I wondered, *'Is it really safe to go through life being so comfortable with danger?'* I didn't know when I should be scared because I was so accustomed to stress and chaos. What else have I become accustomed to that may truly be a danger to me? Just how many bills have I paid with a gun pointed at me?"

In your own way, you too may be comfortable with crisis and stress but not necessarily with taking risks. Risk-taking means initiating *purposeful change* in your life. Risks come with the willingness to change, to behave differently because what you have been doing until now has caused problems in your life. Saying no, talking openly about your feelings, and asking others for what you need are all ways of trusting yourself enough to risk change. At first it may seem as if you are walking a tightrope without a safety net, but with such risks come the rewards of open, honest, and balanced relationships. Guaranteed.

6

Making Decisions
You Can Live With

We have it in our power to begin the world again.
— THOMAS PAINE

How do you confront such dilemmas as whether or not to commit a family member to a hospital, let him live with you, provide for his future, or sign a release for shock treatment? How do you react to threats of violence? How do you handle crises? How do you deal with the stigma surrounding mental illness that is prevalent in our society? When schizophrenia seems to be inherited in your family, how do you decide whether or not to have children? Should you move to another state, leaving your parents alone with your mentally ill sister? Many people approach such decisions with the sense that there are only one or two solutions. They don't realize that it is their own inner feelings of fear and self-doubt that prevent

them from recognizing that there are always many alternatives.

THE DEMONS OF DECISIONS

Decisions are often frightening. We often think of highly
imaginative ways to avoid making a decision, or we may prefer
to let others decide for us. We are frightened by the power
implicit in making a decision and also fear it will lock us into
something we may later regret. Sometimes, we hesitate to
make decisions because we don't want to be held accountable
for having made a poor one. The need to make a decision can
keep us from our sleep. But in reality it is not the decision
that is the beast but our inner dialogue of fears and concerns
that keeps us up at night. When we give into such resistance
and fear around choices, we lose our ability to be the director
of our own lives. *Not* making a decision actively is still a
choice. This choice will still have consequences.

Before you confront any *outer* crises or decisions in your
life, you must first confront your inner demons—the shame,
fear, judgmentalness, and self-doubt within you that limit your
choices by limiting your creation of alternatives. Fears, shame,
judgmentalness, self-doubt, and guilt weaken the creative
process. If you feel guilty and base a decision on this guilt, or
react out of fear, you are shutting out the many other possibilities available to you. Dealing with crises and dilemmas with
these inner demons blocking the way is like putting out a blaz-
ing fire with fire. You simply add to the flame of indecision.

Bev has to make a decision about whether or not to let
her sister live with her. Although the decisions you confront
may be more or less difficult, she is dealing with the same
inner demons that you do as she tries to decide. Bev's sister,
Lorraine, has been diagnosed as having a borderline personality disorder. She cuts her arms and upper legs with a
razor when she is angry or frustrated, and refuses to stay on
her medication, going off it every time her condition

begins to stabilize. Their mother can no longer care for Lorraine. At age sixty-three, she is disabled from arthritis and needs constant medical attention herself. Bev is thirty-seven and has a husband and two children. She is torn between her concern for her sister and mother and her need to care for herself and her family. She feels she has only two choices: to let her sister live with her and expect her family to handle the stress, or to let her sister fend for herself. Bev fears that Lorraine will end up in another abusive relationship, which has happened numerous times before when she has moved out on her own. Bev is torn between her guilt and her fears, and doesn't feel good about either of these choices.

Like most of us, Bev's decision is determined by the alternatives she believes are available to her. She doesn't realize that her inner demons of guilt and fear are blocking her from considering additional ways to solve her problem and that it is her lack of alternatives that is causing her suffering. There are several inner demons consistently identified by those close to the mentally ill. The need to make a decision can provide an opportunity for you to meet your own inner demons face to face, to identify them and understand what is getting in the way of decisions you can live with.

THE INNER DEMON OF SHAME

Due largely to overly dramatic film and television portrayals of mental illness and to other biased representations, most people view the mentally ill as beyond help, unable to live normal lives. Often, they are assumed to be murderers and psychopaths. Because of these widespread misconceptions, it is understandable that family members are reluctant to tell others about their mentally ill loved one and feel ashamed about having mental illness in their family.

Gloria felt more and more uncomfortable with the discussion her friends were having about the article in the morning paper. Some man had gone on a rampage and killed three pedestrians on the sidewalk. In the article it was mentioned that his wife had recently died of leukemia and that he was presently unemployed. He also had a "brief psychiatric history." The headline for the story was: SCHIZOPHRENIC KILLS THREE PEDESTRIANS. Gloria listened to her friends expressing their fears about "crazy people," and asking "How do people like that get out of the hospital, anyway?" The conversation turned to the movie *Psycho* and how close that movie must be to reality. Gloria fell silent, thinking about her last trip to the state hospital to visit her brother, Seth. She had met with the doctors, who told her that Seth might be ready to go home soon. Which meant to Gloria that she would have to fight hard to keep her secret about Seth from her friends. She sat there listening to them talk, feeling more and more alone.

Family members of the mentally ill constantly bump up against similar misconceptions and prejudices. In fact, before the Rude Awakening described in Chapter 1, family members also believed the widely shared myths about mental illness. Not until the mental illness was openly accepted and confronted did they come to understand it. On the one hand, family members can empathize with those who still hold misconceptions about mental illness; on the other hand, they are stigmatized by these very misconceptions.

When we internalize the ignorance of the general public, when we learn not to disclose our concerns to others for fear of being judged mentally ill or "strange" ourselves, we begin to believe that there is something bad within our families and ourselves, and we experience shame. As a result, we create distance between ourselves and others. Because intimacy includes the willingness and ability to open up to others; without self-disclosure, friendships and intimate relationships are impoverished.

Victor, an accountant for a large firm in New York, has a sister, Lindsay, who has been diagnosed with several mental illnesses. She was first hospitalized when she was sixteen and Victor was seventeen. He is now thirty-four and lives several hundred miles from Lindsay. He recalls the times when he would feel defensive when acquaintances referred to "crazy people" in a derogatory way. When others spoke of mental illness jokingly, he took it personally. However, he kept his feelings to himself and never told others that he had a sister who was mentally ill. No one at work knew about his sister; in fact, he generally acted as if he didn't have a sister. He was alienated by others' misconceptions and angered at himself for behaving as if his sister were dead. As he explains, "I was unwilling to tell others about my sister because I felt they would think there was something wrong with *me*. Even today I am very selective about whom I share this with, and my fiancée didn't even know I had a sister till about six months after we began dating."

It is Victor's own sense of shame that causes him to feel as if others are attacking him when they talk insensitively about mental illness. Because he too shares many of the misconceptions about mental illness, he is unable to confront the social stigma that surrounds him. He admits to not knowing for certain whether he and his family are all "crazy." And the farther he distances himself from others, the more "crazy" he feels.

Shame has many layers and causes. Shame, unlike guilt, is a feeling we have about *ourselves*, that we are bad, dirty, sinful, wrong. Whereas guilt is more about feelings we have around our *behaviors*: "I felt guilty not calling my father on his birthday." Victor in the above story feels shame—that something is wrong with him because of the mental illness in the family. Later in Victor's own healing process he discovered his shame went deeper than just dealing with his sister's mental illness. His father was very abusive and his mother a passive bystander. Victor remembers witnessing his father sexually abuse his sister when she was five years old. Such abuse causes deep-seated layers of shame because children internalize any abuse. They assume they are being abused because they are bad, wrong, dirty, evil. This internalized shame is then buried, coming out later in our adult lives as feelings of shame.

Shame can also be the result of being "shamed" by others for not behaving a certain way. Too many parents use shaming statements to control their children's behaviors. Again, these statements are then internalized by the child and become *feelings* of shame within the adult. Shame is a double-edged sword; it keeps you from opening up to others and this isolation increases your shame.

Shame means telling yourself things like:

"If anyone knew about the mental illness in my family, he would think there was something wrong with me."
"There *is* something wrong with me."
"I'm going to get discovered for the bad/stupid/dirty person I really am."
"My friends will be afraid of me if I tell them about my family."
"No one will want to have children with me because of the mental illness."
"I can't show my feelings because others will think I am crazy too. "
"I must never be dependent on others because that is a sign of weakness, of mental illness."
"When people discover the real me, they won't like me."

Shame is a negative perception we hold of ourselves. We can only feel ashamed of what we believe to be true about ourselves and our families. Shame also internalizes the social stigma and interferes with how we make decisions because we react to our feelings of shame rather than the decision confronting us. We *feel* shameful and therefore we *act* ashamed.

Many family members believe, for example, that they have somehow contributed to the mental illness. Parents often assume they somehow caused the illness, while siblings, spouses, and adult children agonize over ways they could have prevented it. These assumptions create feelings of shame about themselves and their families.

However, *stigma* is real and the many misconceptions about mental illness are not likely to change overnight. Fortunately, we can change even if, until now, we have allowed our lives to be governed by shame and fear of ostracism; by learning more about ourselves and about mental illness we can overcome our shame. By working on the Eight Stage Healing Process, we can bring about balance in our lives. We can heal the many causes and layers of our shame, whatever they may be.

Truth Serum

To begin overcoming feelings of shame, start with a brief evaluation of your own beliefs about and reactions to the mental illness (Stage 1 and 2). If you are embarrassed or hurt by what others say, it is because you accept that what they say is true. You will be less at the mercy of others' opinions and more secure about your own feelings and beliefs about mental illness after taking a closer look at your own assumptions and feelings.

Can you then, with the help of a therapist or group take a more honest look at your family history and relationships? Was there any abuse in the family? Just where does your feelings of shame come from? Were there shaming comments made to you and others in the family? *Secrecy feeds shame.* Breaking the silence around our experiences and feelings, gradually frees us from shame. Don't feed the flame of shame with more secrets—*talk about what happened.* If your shame is about the mental illness, break the shame-cycle of secrecy and share your experiences and thoughts with others.

Make Your Point Through Gentle Advocacy

Our improved sense of self-worth and awareness can help to eradicate the stigma associated with mental illness because how we react to our loved one's mental illness affects the community's reaction to the illness. When we react with shame, others assume there is something to be ashamed about. So long as we keep mental illness a secret, the community cannot learn the truth about mental illness and its effects on families.

If, for example, you believe mental illness is caused by poor communication between parents, you may blame your parents for causing the mental illness. Such a belief also reflects how you think others perceive the mental illness and your family. If you believe that mentally ill people are "evil" and "possessed," this will affect how you react to the mentally ill person and the reactions you anticipate from others. If you believe you and your family have a terrible secret to hide, this will cause you to feel shame when others talk ignorantly about mental illness. For further discussion on challenging your beliefs, see Stage Four of the Eight Stages, found in Chapter 8.

Gentle advocacy is one way to battle stigma, instead of allowing the stigma to distance you from others. Through gentle advocacy you can educate the public about mental illness and the effects it has on the family, without taking personally the comments or responses of other people.

Gentle advocacy means sharing information and insight about mental illness on a one-to-one basis rather than through large groups or demonstrations. Because it does not have the aggressive edge that some forms of advocacy take it permits you to be involved with people who hold different views, and gives you the opportunity to educate and influence the public's beliefs about mental illness at the same time. With this style of advocacy you can choose whether or not you want to share your personal story. Until you are ready to deal with inevitably ignorant and intolerant reactions it would be wise to choose your confidants carefully. Furthermore, when telling others that you have a family member with mental illness, instead of calling it mental illness or schizophrenia you may want to say something like, "My sister has a brain disorder." This emphasizes the dis-ease rather than triggering the many misconceptions that surround such labels as "schizo-phrenia," and "mental illness."

Empathy is a valuable aspect of gentle advocacy. It involves understanding that the other person has misconceptions about mental illness primarily because he hasn't been taught anything else. One way to be understanding is to keep in mind the biases you once held. Imagine yourself as a teacher and give others time to unlearn the myths they hold about mental illness; then you can help educate them about the facts of mental illness. It can be difficult to remain calm and empathetic while someone is teasing or putting down a mentally ill person, but tolerating differences allows others to open up. They are then more likely to take the time to listen to what you have to say.

THE INNER DEMON OF GUILT

The next demon to bring out into the light is the fear you may have of carrying a lifelong responsibility for your mentally ill relative/friend, a common concern among siblings and adult children of the mentally ill.

The story of Roberta's family demonstrates how this fear affects every family member: Roberta remembers the difficulty her younger brother Sam had in his freshman year of college. He was not adjusting to being away from home and did not seem to fit in on campus. Sam often made the thirty-mile drive to visit Roberta, confiding in her the difficulties he was undergoing. He spoke of voices whispering to him and of his special plan to convert the campus religiously; he also spoke of the many ways a person could kill himself. He talked a lot about death and suicide. Roberta contacted the campus counselors and they advised her to bring him home. Roberta helped Sam pack and move back in with their parents. He soon settled into a familiar pattern of sleeping, hiding in his room, and drawing dark pictures in charcoal of people with heads of animals. Only occasionally would he come out of his room to eat a meal with his parents.

The longer Sam remained at home, the more dependent he became on the safety it provided. He once left to live in a supervised apartment program only to return home every weekend. After three months in the program he was ousted for smoking marijuana with two other residents. He then moved back with his parents. Roberta was frightened by Sam's progressive dependency and reliance on his parents. During Roberta's fourth year at college, she visited home only once, during Yom Kippur. The discomfort of that visit six months ago still upsets her. Her parents seem to have grown older and more tired from the continuing trauma of Sam's illness.

It was during her visit on Yom Kippur that Roberta became aware of her fear: that someday Sam would be dependent on her, causing her to lose a measure of freedom. What future is there for those who, like Roberta, are expected to continue providing care for a mentally ill relative? The fear of this responsibility can permeate one's life, shaping major life decisions regarding marriage, children, education, and career.

Don't Live in the Future

It is the parents who set the stage for what kind of relationships others in the family will have with the mentally ill member and with each other. Families need to encourage as much autonomy in the mentally ill person as possible. Siblings and children of the mentally ill will have less fear for their future and the future of their mentally ill relative when they know that everything is being done to promote independence. Although worrying about the future won't help, planning for the future is wise.

If you are a parent, you have a significant influence on how your family prepares for the future. You need to take a careful look at how you are providing for your mentally ill son or daughter and to discuss what you expect from other family members for the future care of your mentally ill child.

If parents are not including others in the decision-making process, or are unwilling to consider alternatives to home care, the family members most affected will have to speak up. After all, it is also their future that is being shaped by parental decisions. Make it clear that plans for your mentally ill relative's treatment, housing, or care affect you. Don't silently agree to provide for your mentally ill loved one. Don't *silently* agree to anything. Furthermore, make sure you have enough information about the options available—in this case guardianships, wills, and trusts—to influence the decisions now being made. As mentioned earlier, speaking up may produce conflict, but through this conflict a more cooperative solution can be built. The options of guardianships, wills and trusts are mentioned briefly below.

Guardianship is a legal relationship requiring sanction by an appointed panel or the court. Its purpose is to protect the mentally ill person. Each state has its own guardianship laws which will determine the steps to take and what is available. If it is legally established that a mentally ill person is unable to make decisions in his own best interest, a guardianship may be set up to give this responsibility to someone else. Public or private organizations, family members, friends, or agencies can all be designated as guardians. If you become a guardian, you have the right and duty to act on behalf of your mentally ill relative.

The question to ask if you are considering being a guardian is how much protection does your mentally ill family member require? There are different types of guardianship agreements, including a "guardianship of property," in which specific areas of responsibility are agreed upon by the family and the court.

For anyone interested in arranging a guardianship, the first step is to seek the advice of an attorney who has a solid knowledge of family law. In addition, you will want to make sure that guardianship is the best way to protect the future of the mentally ill family member; a will or trust may be a better option. It is worthwhile for the family to investigate all the possibilities available before making a decision.

Relatives of the mentally ill often avoid discussing the possibility of drawing up a will because it brings to mind the reality of death and may lead to increased anxiety regarding the future of the mentally ill person. This is regrettable because having to plan for the mentally ill loved one can cause the family even more stress if the family's provider dies without leaving a will.

Families who are concerned about the future needs and security of a mentally ill loved one should not postpone discussing and writing a will. Such questions as how and what to will to the mentally ill family member, financial guardianship, and financial security can be addressed in a will. Again, it is important to include everyone in the family in assessing the purpose of the agreements in the will.

A **trust** can be the most practical method of providing for the long-term care of a mentally ill family member. Trusts are as legally binding as wills and guardianships and may be better suited to the special predicaments of the mentally ill family member. With a trust, one individual, the trustee, manages the assets and property of the disabled person according to a written agreement drawn up by the creator of the trust. The beneficiary of the trust, the mentally ill person in this case, receives all the assets according to the agreement. The trustee does not hold any power over how the money is allocated or spent. Therefore, the mentally ill person has more autonomy.

To further conquer this fear of future responsibility, continue to create an internal separation between you and the mentally ill member as mentioned in the previous chapter. Your needs, desires, and future are of great value too and there is no reason whatsoever that you must put your life plans aside to care for another. However, providing care for another is something you can freely choose to do.

Planning for the future is healthy, and make certain your future plans include your dreams and goals as well. It is just as important however not to be *focused* on the future but to be present for the experiences and decisions you have before you now.

Calming the Worrying Mind

The worrying mind can cause more stress and suffering than any external circumstance. Therefore, having skills in stilling the mind, calming our worried thoughts can be of great benefit. Mindfulness meditation, also known as awareness mediation, or Vipassana, is such a tool.

Meditation can help you break through the endless internal dialogue of worries, negative thinking, judgmental comments of self and others—breaking through to *experiencing the reality* of the present. Sometimes experiencing the reality of the present means accepting difficult and painful feelings and circumstances. This can be done without losing our serenity, without giving up our inner calm. And mindfulness meditation offers us this alternative.

A Guided Meditation

This can be taped and played back to you, read aloud in a group, or by a friend.

Sit comfortably in an alert position, with the back comfortably straight but not arched or rigid. Try not to be too relaxed so that your back is leaning against the back of a chair. Instead, softly rest your lower back against the chair or a pillow. Have your legs uncrossed and feet flat on the floor.

Bring your awareness into this time and place, into the room. Let the events of the day, the week, the future drop away. Do this by bringing your awareness to your body as it sits in the chair. Notice the sensations of your body as it sits—your feet upon the floor, how your arms are positioned, your torso as it presses against the chair. Allow your shoulders to drop down slightly, to relax. Allow your jaw to relax by letting your mouth be slightly opened. Notice any other sensations that may be in the body, places of warmth or cold, tension or calmness. Without judgment or thought, bring simple awareness to your various body sensations by just noticing the various sensations that are happening in your body.

Now let the breath breathe by itself, naturally, without any control of it.

Bring your awareness to the place where your breath enters and leaves the body, which is along the top of your nostrils. Place your awareness there, softly.

Notice the sensations that arise and fall as you breathe in and breathe out. Allowing the breath to breathe by itself, keeping your awareness, softly focused on the breath as it moves in and moves out.

Keep your attention, your awareness on the breath.

When you find your awareness has moved to another body sensation, a thought, a worry, a tingling somewhere, simply notice where your attention has gone and gently and lovingly—softly—bring it back to the breath.

Watch the breath as it moves in and out, naturally at the top of the nostrils. You may want to label the breaths: "inward"(on the in breath) and "outward" (on the out breath). Do this without having your focus on the words; let the words be a reminder where your attention is—on the in and out movement of the breath. Just be with the sensations of the breath as it naturally, without effort, moves in and moves out.

Thoughts will arise, feelings, sensations. Just allow them to rise and fall, to pass away as background to the breath. Always returning your attention to the breath as it moves in and moves out. Moves in and moves out.

Do not hold on to a thought, do not follow its' story to conclusion. Return to the breath. You are learning to not grasp at thought, at worry. Mindful of the breathing, not grasping or avoiding. Just soft observation of the breath as it moves in and moves out.

Each breath unique, natural. Focus on the whole breath as it moves out and moves in. Your focus is on the sensations of breathing in and breathing out. No "thinking." Just breath and the sensations of breath. Feeling the breath brush past your nostrils as it moves in and moves out. Everything outside of the breath— thought, other body sen-

sations—are outside the focus of your meditation. *The object of your meditation, of your awareness is the sensations of your breath. Watching your breath, slowly as it moves in and moves out.*

Don't wonder off in thought. If the mind wanders off, gently, without judgment, return to the breath. Notice the entire breath from its beginning to its end. Again, the object of your meditation is the sensations of the breath as it moves in and moves out.

The body breathes by itself, without effort. Your awareness simply, without force observes the breath as it moves in and out.

Each breath completely new. Each moment completely new. Letting the old breath go; allowing the new breath in, without effort. You simply, softly focus your awareness on the breath.

Moment to moment, simply watching the breath. Moment to moment, watching what arises and what falls. Everything changes, like the breath—it rises and falls, it moves into your life and then out. Everything passes. Everything. Nothing remains: the sun as it moves across your face, the thought you just had, the first tulip of spring, the morning star, all passes.

Pure awareness is free of "Thinking." It's like the sun shinning through a window; where the light lands is awareness. Through practicing awareness meditation we gradually learn to be like the light shining through the window, bringing light to what is, free of worry, judgment, and negative thoughts. Commit to doing five minutes of mindfulness meditation a day, preferably first thing in the morning. Begin gradually, with only five minutes. This is enough. The goal is to have the practice of meditation be part of your life, not to sit for long periods of time.

For more guidance on Mindfulness meditation there are many excellent books available, listed below are a few suggestions:

<u>Minding the Body: Mending the Mind</u>
by Joan Borysenko, Ph. D., Bantam Books

<u>Full Catastrophe Living: Using the Wisdom of Your Body and Mind to Face Stress, Pain and Illness</u>
by Jon Kabat-Zinn, Ph. D., Dell publishing

<u>Guided Meditations, Explorations and Healings</u>
by Stephen Levine., Anchor Books

The Final Good-bye to Guilt

Guilt is often expressed by words like "should," "ought," or "must." Guilt originates with such thoughts as "It could have been me" or "I have it so good and she has it so bad." Guilt can easily lead to the assumption that you owe it to another to do something, and that if you don't, you are unkind. Guilt is often accompanied by the belief that you are somehow responsible for another's life.

Of course it is normal to experience guilt when you have harmed others by some destructive or abusive act, or have ignored someone in need, but it is unhealthy when you allow guilt to determine your behavior toward others. When you are motivated by the desire to subdue your guilt, solving a problem becomes much more difficult.

Instead of reacting to such feelings and beliefs, you can *take the time to decide* what you want to do in a given situation. Do not allow guilt to compel you to make limited choices; instead, consider your many alternatives.

THE FEAR OF INHERITING MENTAL ILLNESS: ANOTHER INNER DEMON

The fear of either having a breakdown or having children who become mentally ill haunts many spouses, siblings, and adult children of the mentally ill. This fear can have a detrimental effect on their emotional well-being and can affect their decision about whether or not to have children. If they are constantly searching for signs of mental illness within themselves, this preoccupation will inhibit them from making many important life decisions freely.

> "My biggest fear? That's an easy one—it's always been that I too may become mentally ill, that some dark spot in me will open up and I will forever be sick like my mother. But now that I'm past the age when my mother first got sick, I am beginning to wonder whether or not I should have children. Would I pass some defective gene on to them? I've never shared this with anyone, not even my husband, but I worry a lot about having children."

At one time or another most siblings and adult children of the mentally ill have wondered about their own vulnerability to mental illness. For siblings the fear that they too may be mentally ill usually comes up during adolescence. Adult children of the mentally ill live with the fear of becoming mentally ill well into their later years. More often than not, the fear of inheriting mental illness subsides once the age is passed where the vulnerability seems most apparent, which is when their relative became ill. However, this fear often gives way to a fear about the possibility of passing mental illness on to their children.

> "My mother had manic-depression. I have lived with her illness all my life. We both suffered terribly. She wasn't treated for her condition until I was seventeen. Finally our lives calmed down. And although I haven't shown signs of manic-depression myself, I worry about my two beautiful children. I can't bear the thought of them suffering through their lives as my mother did. I sometimes wonder if it was fair for me to have had children. I just wish there was something I could do to guarantee that they would be okay. But of course there isn't."

As another daughter who has a father with schizophrenia pointed out in a support group for siblings and adult children of the mentally ill, "Have you noticed that most of us are married but none of us has children?"

Choosing To Have Children

Educating oneself about the genetic basis of mental illness and getting genetic counseling are two solutions for those concerned about the heritability of mental illness.

The lifelong risk of developing the dis-ease schizophrenia is about one in one hundred for the general population. However, the actual risk is greatest between the ages of fifteen and twenty-five. This risk decreases significantly after the age of forty. Research has determined that those with one brother or sister with mental illness have about a seven to ten percent chance of developing the same mental illness. In comparison, an adult child with one schizophrenic parent has a ten to thirteen percent chance of developing the disorder.

While many of the major mental illnesses may have a biological basis, other factors determine the risk of actually developing a mental illness. These factors may include improper nutrition, environmental stress, such as family abuse, or the ingestion of street drugs such as hallucinogens or cocaine. Moreover, a given person's mental illness is likely to have more than one contributing factor. For example, schizophrenia due to a defect in a single gene is rare; as few as one in ten thousand cases may be identified as purely genetic in basis. Likewise, schizophrenia due solely to environmental factors may also be rare. The risks will vary significantly from individual to individual and family to family, depending on the factors in each case. However, the news may be more positive than you expect. For those considering children, psychiatric genetic counseling is recommended.

Psychiatric genetic counseling can assist you in predicting the risk you or your children have of contracting mental illness. However, the procedures currently used in screening for the risk of mental illness are not one hundred percent accurate. Unlike Down's syndrome, schizophrenia and manic-depression cannot yet be traced to a specific chromosomal malformation, although recent data reveal that manic-depression does have a genetic factor. Counseling will, therefore, increase your understanding of your present and potential risk. In addition, it may be a valuable educational tool.

Most teaching hospitals connected with large universities have genetic counselors and a psychiatric staff that would be able to do a comprehensive evaluation for you.

Even if you receive a low risk estimate of passing on mental illness, you may still be troubled by the *fear* of having a child who becomes mentally ill. When the likelihood of inheritance is small, it is important not to make decisions based on your fears, but rather to fully explore your *desires*—which may or may not include being a parent. Call on your inner faith to guide you. Also, providing a healthy, loving environment for a child will certainly contribute significantly to his or her well-being.

THE FEAR OF ABANDONMENT

Siblings and adult children easily recall the time their brother, sister, or parent began showing drastic character changes. Many view this as they would the death of a loved one. As one adult child says, "It's as if my father left, never to return, and a stranger took his place . . . a stranger who doesn't laugh and talks about frightening things." The fear of loss is the fear of a repetition of the sense of abandonment you experienced when your family member became mentally ill.

Loss is stressful and frightening, and must be dealt with in order to overcome the fear of abandonment. As discussed in Chapter 1, the feelings of anger, grief, and fear that accompany this loss are not openly recognized by the family. The silent agreement here is to remain quiet with your pain, so as to keep peace within the family. *The family's inability to mourn its loss serves only to intensify the loss.*

If you have an underlying fear of abandonment, it is bound to interfere with your ability to trust, make commitments, and form satisfying relationships. Your decisions may be directed by a fear of loss if you have such thoughts as:

"This relationship won't last."
"I can't make long-term commitments."
"He's going to leave me when he finds out more about me."
"I can't stand it when she's gone."
"I have always been alone, I like it this way."
"I have no idea how to maintain an intimate relationship."

If someone close to you has committed suicide, it is likely that your fears of abandonment are even more intense. So long as you are protecting yourself by denying the profound effect of the suicide, overcoming your fear will be next to impossible.

Jenny still denies the feelings she has regarding her brother's suicide: "I loved my brother, Roger. He always took care of me. My family had a lot of problems and he was my mainstay in life. Even after he became ill with schizophrenia he still tried to protect me. He always wanted to be with me. We tried to keep the same relationship we had before his illness but we couldn't do it. The playfulness and the spontaneity were gone. He was so gloomy and paranoid. I always worried that one day he would commit suicide. Sometimes when he disappeared I would search for him. And one weekend I couldn't find him. He was only thirty-one when he killed himself. But at least he is at peace. I've never really felt sad because he is probably happier dead. I believe he is at peace now, so why should I be unhappy?"

This was the most significant person in Jenny's life, yet she claims she has accepted his suicide simply because *"he is at peace."* The one person she claims really loved her committed suicide, but she denies she is angry or sad.

Jenny has never had a long-term relationship with another

person, stating that she prefers to live a "private life." Now, even after Roger is dead, Jenny continues to avoid her own feelings of grief and anger and her fear of abandonment. In many ways, she is still caretaking her dead brother by ignoring her own feelings. Roger may be at peace, but what about how she feels, what about the relationship that meant so much to her? Her decision to remain outside intimate relationships is dictated by her fear of abandonment. Her distrust of others. Until she admits her fears, and develops enough courage to love again, Jenny will continue to seclude herself. Until she opens the door to her feelings she will continue pretending that everything is fine because "he is at peace."

Mourn Your Losses

Don't let your feelings and thoughts about your loss turn into demons by keeping them secret. Acknowledge your feelings (Stage 2). Talk to your family and others about the changes that have occurred since your friend or relative became ill or committed suicide. Give yourself and others permission to express such feelings as anger, fear, sadness, and confusion without fear of being judged. Learn to accept the loss of how the person once behaved and the relationship as it was. If he or she is still alive, this acceptance makes it possible for you to develop a new relationship with the mentally ill person. Every relationship changes as a result of the mental illness, so make certain to discuss how the change affects you (Stage 1). Finally, give yourself and others time to adapt to the mental illness or death.

THE THREAT OF VIOLENCE: A REAL DEMON

Because of the stigma families are battling—that mentally ill people are dangerous, sociopathic, and unable to live normal lives—violence that *does* occur in these families is often kept a secret. Two types of violence exist in families with mental illness: actual physical abuse and "psychological violence."

Psychological violence means living with threats of physical violence. Physical abuse within families of the mentally ill may not be no more common than in other families, but psychological violence is quite common and is often initiated by the mentally ill person.

Typically today's parents were raised in families where no one talked about problems, especially alcoholism or behavioral problems. Hence, parents are probably uncertain how to deal with the threats and prefer to leave such skeletons in the closet. No one openly talks about the verbal abuse. Indeed, families cope with the fear of violence by making still another silent agreement. As a result the family is living in a threatening environment but no one is doing anything about it.

Such statements as, "He can't help it, he's ill," "He won't hurt you, he's just threatening, " or "Just stay away from her when she gets that way," all discount the genuine fear that is experienced by the person being threatened. His fear is real but he is being told by others "not to worry, it's no big deal." The home, the place one is supposed to feel safe, becomes the place one fears and often avoids. This creates a pattern of coping that endangers family members: *they learn to tolerate abusive behaviors in others*. Many siblings and adult children lack the skills necessary in accurately assessing the safety of a relationship. Their tolerant level of abuse and threatening behavior is too high. Therefore, they often find themselves in dangerous relationships with abusive people. An important part of their healing process includes teaching them to be intolerant of abuse. No one has to tolerate abuse. Mental illness does not excuse someone to be abusive to others.

You may be like Laura, who still lives in fear of her father: "I used to hide in the attic because the latch could be taken off, making it impossible for my father to open the door. He never found me when I hid there. Although I was safe from him, it was a dark and lonely place to hide. My father was a loud and frightening man. He was never diagnosed as having a mental illness but I now believe he suffered from manic-depression. Many things were broken in our home. It was an unhappy, frightening place to be. My mother couldn't control him because she was usually intoxicated. I'm twenty-seven years old now and I am still afraid of my father. I am afraid of a lot of things, and I am angry, too. Angry that my life has been terribly disrupted by my father's abusive threats. Angry that my mother continues to drink and my father still lashes out at my one brother, who lives at home. Mostly, I am angry that I have so much hurt inside of me to heal before I am capable of being in a relationship with a man."

For Laura, her whole life is like hiding out in a dark and lonely attic to which she has removed the door latch.

When you live with psychological violence you begin to develop coping skills that guard you and put a distance between you and the danger. As an adult, you make decisions as if you are still in danger, much as Laura does in the above story. It's also possible to adapt yourself too well to living with psychological violence. If your feelings of fear and concern are not validated by the rest of your family, you may have a difficult time discerning what is truly safe and what is not. You may be drawn into other relationships in which verbal abuse is "acceptable" because it is familiar.

Sara describes how she used to go to her mother about the threats her brother made against her. She recalls having many dreams in which her brother attempted to kill her: "Once I dreamed that my brother had burned me by pushing me against a hot oven and had stabbed me with a kitchen knife. The knife was still in my stomach when my mother came home from getting groceries. She couldn't see that I was dying, that I had a knife in my stomach. *She just stood there talking about groceries while I was dying.*"

Just as in her dream, no one in Sara's family notices that she feels she is in danger. She is walking around with a knife in her stomach but no one seems to care. Sara's mother is confused about the problem and simply hopes it will pass. So, to cope, Sara will either learn to protect herself or become accustomed to abuse.

Protect Yourself at All Times

If you are presently in a relationship in which someone is verbally or physically abusing you, ask yourself why. Is it because the person can't control his emotions and this is acceptable to you? Is it because you have never known anything else? Are you living with parents who expect you to live with these behaviors? Are you keeping it a secret too? Do you believe that you somehow *deserve* to be treated this way? Do you assume that there is nothing you can do about it anyway, so why try?

No one ever has to remain in an abusive relationship. Do not wait for others to make the environment safe for you if those around you are not discussing the psychological violence in your family. In that case, it is up to you to make it safe for yourself. If you are living with your family and it is a parent or sibling who is abusive, *go outside the home for help if necessary.* Tell someone that you are either being abused or that you are afraid of the possibility of abuse.

The threat of violence can be used as a means of manipulation. The mentally ill person is controlling the family when family members respond to threats with fear and compliance. If the threats do not work, if family members are not manipulated, the mentally ill person will have to try other, perhaps healthier, means to get what he wants. However, manipulation is not the only reason the mentally ill threaten family members and it is important to understand why they may make threats.

When a mentally ill person is psychotic he is usually fearful of most everyone and everything. Anyone experiencing a state of psychosis is living in his own world of delusions and hallucinations. Voices may be talking to him from inanimate objects, usually with foreboding news; walls and furniture may seem to be closing in on him; peoples' faces look hideous, and nothing is familiar. He is in a strange place, occupied by unfamiliar people.

> "My brother, Ron, would pace back and forth in the corner of the front hallway. His eyes would be on the floor and sometimes he would whisper to himself. He wouldn't eat or sleep and soon his skin would turn pale and his pacing would increase. If I approached him, he would threaten to rip my face off. Even though I was scared, he seemed more frightened than I was. Once he told me what it was like for him when he became psychotic: 'Everyone wore Indian war paint and I couldn't escape the feeling that the world was going to end. Everyone could read my thoughts and sometimes I could read theirs. Death was everywhere. I was in a strange country and no one was familiar to me.' "

Frightened people will often strike out to defend themselves. Often, those who are psychotic will aggressively protect themselves from what they consider to be dangerous encounters .

Other reasons that the mentally ill family member may become aggressive or abusive include:

- The family often challenges the individual's delusional thinking. In response, the mentally ill person may feel forced to defend his delusions, which can cause him to react defensively or abusively.
- Normal dynamics among family members, such as sibling rivalry and jealousy, may be magnified and distorted by the mentally ill person.
- The mentally ill are more vulnerable to stress and more easily irritated by family interactions and expectations.
- The social isolation that most mentally ill persons experience can lead to dependency on the family. This dependency increases the stress between them and the family, and it

is not surprising that their delusions usually involve family members.

- When a family member takes on the role of Caretaker, family relationships change. The mentally ill member may feel patronized or humiliated, and resent this new relationship.

Typically, the mentally ill strike out at those with whom they are most intimate, usually their family. However, when removed from the home environment, they often no longer act in an abusive or threatening way. This may be in part because those outside the family are more likely to set limits and are less willing to put up with abusive behavior. However, family members and the mentally ill person can learn to identify the warning signs that precede a psychotic episode and can take preventive measures. This will permit families to create a safe environment in which the fear of violence does not inhibit problem-solving.

When Life Becomes a Series of Habits

Much of life is habit. Everyone engages in negative and positive habits. Negative habits, like smoking cigarettes, ruminating on past mistakes, or overeating, are harmful and self-defeating, but they remain intact primarily because of the inner demons which are still living and breeding within us. These inner demons of fear, self-doubt, and shame can also be habitual ways to react to dilemmas. In contrast, positive habits, like buckling your seat belt or meditating every morning, protect or enhance your well-being and are supported by positive thoughts. Generally, it is good to be aware of negative habits and habitual thinking patterns because of their power to block creative problem solving. The expression "I have always done it this way" is a sure sign you are reacting out of habit rather than choice.

Other blocks to imaginative problem-solving include:

- Fear of being criticized
- Fear of making mistakes
- Fear of loss of control
- Fear of exposing silent agreements
- Fear of change/taking risks
- Fear of rejection and withdrawal of appreciation from others.

However painful it is to discover one's inner demons, it is destructive to ignore them. Before you can open up to a new life with relationships and experiences that have been, up till now, out of reach, these demons must be identified and conquered. Only then will you be able to make clear decisions and take the first step in creative problem-solving. Once you have vanquished your inner demons, you are free to approach the outer ones. Take the risk in approaching your life and problems differently. Remember: *if you always do what you always did; you'll always get what you always got.*

IMAGINATIVE PROBLEM-SOLVING

Sometimes the outer demons—repeated hospitalizations, lack of social services, psychotic behaviors, violent outbursts, suicide, or refusal of treatment—are so overwhelming that family members feel fortunate if they can simply endure these problems. Imaginative problem-solving is regarded as a time-consuming luxury. However, if you do not take the time to solve your problems creatively, you will continue to react to life, feeling like a person on a roller-coaster ride. Unlike the roller coaster rides at the fair, however, the one you are on will never end. Because you are faced with many important decisions that profoundly affect your life, imaginative problem-solving is a lifesaver, not a luxury.

Paul has so far been living his life on a roller coaster: "Doug was knocking at my door at three in the morning asking me to let him in. I had my fiancee over that evening.

I hadn't any time to decide what to do. Although I admit I considered not opening the door, I couldn't ignore him, so I let him into the hallway. He was obviously on his way to being psychotic. His voice and the expression of fright and confusion on his face always give him away. I looked over at my fiancee, who asked me if I thought she should leave. I was confused. I knew I would be angry with my brother if I let him stay but I would feel guilty if I told him to leave. It seemed I had no choice. If he had called first, I could have told him we could get together tomorrow. But he was standing in my hallway now, so what could I do, kick him out?"

There seems to be an endless list of dilemmas families of the mentally ill are confronted with. Often family members will say, "But in *our* situation there really isn't an alternative," believing that their situation is so unique and troublesome that alternatives simply don't exist. Perhaps you are now facing a problem like one described below:

"Nothing works for my son. We've tried every medication available, and nothing works."

"At every family gathering my brother gets disruptive. We can never get together anymore and relax."

"My mother refuses to stay on her medication. As soon as she starts feeling better she stops taking it. This has been going on since I was nine years old."

"My father left us when I was four. I have no one to help me with my mother and sister, who are both mentally ill. My father will have nothing to do with any of us—not even me. He started another family fifteen years ago and doesn't acknowledge us; we simply don't exist."

"I can't bring myself to sign the release form for shock treatment for my daughter. But the doctors insist that it's the last resort because nothing else has helped pull her out of her depression. I have lived with five years of hearing 'This is the last resort.'"

"My sister married a schizophrenic. She's divorced now, and

she and her daughter have moved in with me and my husband. Now my niece is showing some signs that she may have schizophrenia. This is causing a lot of stress between me and my husband. Just last month we decided to reconsider our decision to have children."

Life is filled with dilemmas. Life also provides clear paths out of them if you can take a creative approach to problem-solving. There are alternatives; you need only to open yourself up to them.

Facing the Real Problem

Your loved one's mental illness may be the heart of the problem, but by now you are probably aware that the relationships within the family are often the problems that most need your attention. To generate alternative solutions to dilemmas that may be a consequence of the mental illness, it will be necessary to widen your focus to include more than just the mental illness. Many families continue to attempt to change the mentally ill person, or accept the mental illness while ignoring related problems. But in fact the actual problem may not even be the mental illness, or the person who is mentally ill. It may be how you are responding to the illness.

Barb believes that if her son simply agrees to take his medication, all their problems will be solved: "Jack just won't take his medication. He thinks that we're trying to hurt him. What can you do when someone is so sick but refuses to take his medication? He won't visit the mental health clinic with me. I guess I just have to live with it. It's Jack and me alone in this big house. I can't force him to get help. I can't make him get well. He doesn't even think he's sick; he says I am trying to destroy him. Our lives would return to normal if he would just take his medication."

In the above example, the mental illness is the mother's

primary concern. Consequently, getting Jack to take his medication is the only solution she recognizes. Right now this solution is unacceptable to Jack. Remove the attention from the mental illness and then what is the problem? The dilemma becomes a set of smaller, perhaps more manageable, problems, including:

- A son who is unwilling to accept that he needs medication
- A mother and son who disagree as to what should be done
- A mother who is feeling totally responsible for her son
- A lack of involvement from other family members
- A son who refuses to visit the mental health clinic
- A son who distrusts his mother's motives

Barb is correct in thinking that she can't force Jack to take his medication but is his refusal to cooperate the only problem here? Like Barb, your first step in imaginative problem-solving is identifying the other problems involved with the dilemma.

The next step is generating alternatives, or brainstorming. When you "brainstorm" your goal is to come up with as many options as possible. Allow your ideas to flow freely. Some of the ideas may not be feasible but that is all right. When generating ideas it is important to be nonjudgmental, to take advantage of the broader perspective of the problem you reached in the first step.

The following alternatives were brainstormed for Barb's dilemma:

- Barb assembles mental health professionals and the family as a group, and they all talk with Jack about his behavior.
- Barb removes herself as the primary decision-maker.
- Barb stops trying to get Jack to take medication.
- Barb seeks outside professional help.
- Barb kicks Jack out of the house.
- Jack is given information about brain dis-eases and medications by those outside the family.

- Barb confronts her feelings of helplessness and guilt.
- Barb and Jack write a contract concerning living arrangements which includes Jack's taking his medication and receiving treatment at the mental health clinic.
- A family contract is written up which involves all family members.
- Barb and Jack seek family counseling.
- If Jack continues to refuse a visit to the mental health clinic, the family will arrange home visits by a social worker or a hospital outreach worker.
- Barb asks other family members to share in the responsibilities regarding her son.

Notice that the solutions above do not focus only on the mental illness or the mentally ill person. *The mental illness no longer stands in the way of solving the dilemma.*

Choosing Alternatives

Now choose the alternatives that are not only practical, but that have consequences that are acceptable to you. Remember, though, that trying new ideas usually feels uncomfortable. Make sure that the inner demons of guilt, fear, and self-doubt are not limiting your choice of alternatives.

To assist you in choosing among your many alternatives consider the following:

- Talk with friends outside the family whose opinions you trust and value.
- Strike from the list the ideas that are unacceptable because they are either harmful or impossible. (For example, at this point, kicking Jack out of the house is unacceptable to Barb.)
- Imagine what the choices will be like, paying attention to any fears or doubts that may arise.

Even after you have made your choices, save your list.

Choices that are not acceptable to you now may be appropriate at a later time.

Putting Your Ideas into Action

While you once were resigned to the problem, you now accept responsibility for solving it—for bringing to life the alternatives you generated and chose. This is the step in which you put your plan into action, in which your needs are met. You now have to get more specific about how you are going to accomplish your plan. Refer to the steps in Chapter Five: Identifying and asking for what you need. You may also want to refer to Stage 8, in Chapter Eight.

Resourceful Crisis Intervention

Often quick decisions are necessary. But even then, you need not act impulsively. Resourcefulness during a crisis means taking whatever time you can to choose among the alternatives.

Once you clearly define the crisis you will be better able to develop resources to handle it effectively and to identify when the crisis is resolved. When a crisis has no boundaries, you are less likely to make productive decisions; instead you will be enmeshed in problems. Although some crises do seem endless, they do not have to govern your life. Especially since mental illness is most often a long-term stress on the family, periods of rest are a necessity.

Therefore, when you find yourself in a crisis, identify and set its *boundaries*, by making clear what is and is not involved in the crisis, as well as what it will take to resolve it. Decide which areas of your life the crisis will affect and which areas will remain unaffected.

Alicia goes off her medication five days before her sister's wedding. Initially, the crisis is described by the family as: *Alicia needs to get back on her medication.* She is already showing signs of increased agitation and irrational and paranoid thinking. Alicia was going to be a bridesmaid and her sister, Janet, is quite upset about the whole event. She is angry and hurt by Alicia's behavior and isn't sure what to do about her wedding plans. Alicia and Janet's parents are more involved in trying to get Alicia into the hospital and on her medication than in the wedding. In fact, Alicia's mother missed a dinner with Janet's future in-laws because Alicia locked herself out of her apartment and needed a key. Janet is not sure how much to tell her new in-laws and is increasingly upset and unsure about what to do. On top of it all, Janet's fiance has never seen Alicia off her medication and Janet is worried about his reaction.

Now put boundaries around the crisis: Decide how far the crisis is going to extend into the lives of those involved. *You* decide on the boundaries of the crisis. Don't allow circumstances or others to dictate this for you.

The following boundaries were established in the situation just described: *The actual crisis is getting Alicia stabilized and on her medication.* This will not involve Janet. Janet can find someone else to take Alicia's place in the ceremony. Alicia, her parents, and her one brother will be responsible for dealing with the crisis, but they will not let it interfere with their involvement with Janet's wedding. Alicia's father will work with her psychiatrist to set up a hospital bed if necessary. Alicia is still stable enough to make some rational choices, so the family is going to hold her accountable for her decisions and mistakes as long as they are not life-threatening. If she locks herself out of her apartment or has some other difficulty, she will have to take care of it herself. Also, Alicia's parents plan to attend the wedding regardless of Alicia's state.

Now the family is in control of the crisis rather than the crisis being in control of them. The crisis, Alicia going off her medication, is not interfering with Janet's wedding because the family has identified the wedding as *outside* the boundaries of the crisis.

Once the family has placed boundaries around the crisis, imaginative problem-solving can be used to address other family issues and concerns that the crisis may have exposed. Furthermore, because the crisis has boundaries and is not affecting every part of their lives, the family can clearly determine when the crisis has been resolved. In this case, the crisis is over when Alicia is either in the hospital and/or stabilized on her medication. After the crisis, the family can sit down together and talk about what happened, take some preventive measures, and continue problem-solving. Most important, when the crisis ends it is time for them to relax, play, and enjoy.

MAKE THE DECISION TO ENJOY YOUR LIFE

Perhaps the most important decision you can make is to enjoy your life. If you have been involved in problems, worried about the future, or concerned about the well-being of someone else, you probably haven't taken much time to enjoy yourself.

There are no last resorts or problems without solutions. There is an end to the roller-coaster ride of crisis and problems. But you must take yourself off the roller coaster by choosing to stop being involved in problems and becoming more involved with life. This may mean reading a novel, writing a poem, visiting with a friend, joining a dance class, taking a hot bath, or eating out at a fine restaurant. It may even mean going on a long vacation where there are no telephones. Whatever it means for you, take time to recognize all that you have accomplished, take a break from your problems, and make the decision to enjoy your life.

7

Breaking the Silence

> *Once we began to realize that the "afflicted person" is not the only affected person, it became clear that for any kind of normalcy to be regained (or gained for the first time) everyone in the family system must be seen as either part of the problem or part of the solution.*
>
> — EARNIE LARSON

Why can't we sit down as a family and talk about our fears and our concerns? Why so many hidden feelings? Why can't we plan for the future, confront the problems, and create solutions that benefit us all? Why can't we break through the silence and secrets and talk with each other?

We keep quiet because we have always done so to avoid feeling uncomfortable. In fact, we often expend a great deal of emotional energy trying to keep secrets and silent agreements intact, energy that could go into rebuilding a family. But to experience *lasting* harmony within the family, the silent agreements that keep *temporary* peace must be broken.

Behind every silent agreement is an assumption about how we *should* behave, feel, or think. Listed below are some of the silent agreements typically kept by families of the mentally ill. These are the kinds of thoughts and feelings that remain unspoken:

"I must stay healthy. I can't cause any more problems, my family can't handle it."

"All the trouble really started when you divorced me and abandoned the kids. Everything would be all right if you would just have hung in there and helped take care of Kerry."

"To get any attention in my family you have to be involved in a crisis."

"My dad's violent outbursts are considered normal. When he gets angry it's always for a 'good reason.' Last time it was because we were out of eggs."

"My husband and I don't talk about it but we are never going to have children because of the mental illness in my family."

"I know my daughter will take care of her brother when we no longer can."

"I don't tell my husband how sick Helen really is because he has enough to worry about."

"I feel crazy when I go home because everybody is acting like nothing is wrong. Since my brother Norm got into treatment and on medication, it's as if there's nothing else to be concerned about."

"If I don't bring anything up we can all enjoy this time together. Last time I started talking about my feelings, everyone got upset with one another. I think it's best just to keep quiet. "

"Keeping quiet is keeping the peace."

"My children don't know this, but I have lost all hope."

"No one talks about the alcohol problems in my family; everyone pretends that Jeff's mental illness is the only problem."

"Henry's mental illness is the cause of all my unhappiness."

"Someone is to blame for the problems/mental illness in our
family. "

"When my mother is having one of her 'episodes' we all tiptoe
around the house."

"I should take care of Anita when my parents no longer can."

"I'll keep my thoughts and concerns to myself."

"Children aren't supposed to get angry with their parents."

What are you silently agreeing to? What secrets are you
keeping? Take a piece of paper and list three secrets or silent
agreements that you are keeping with your family. You may
also want to identify silent agreements you have within other
relationships, such as with your employer or friend. Every
relationship, every encounter, has built into it silent agreements. The question is: *what are you agreeing to?*

We keep our shame, anger, guilt, resentment, fear, and
doubt buried because we know that when we break the silence
there will be some discomfort and most likely some pain.
Often we keep silent agreements because we fear revealing
ourselves more than we fear the "problem." And, up to now,
the problem has been identified as the mental illness or the
mentally ill person. What has already been revealed in the
previous chapters is that the problem is not simply the mental
illness but how we as families respond to the illness. And we
have responded with painful silence.

"I know what our silent agreement is: My wife and I agree
not to tell our other children when things are getting difficult at home. When they call and ask how we are, I say, 'Just
fine.' Most times, everything is not fine. But I don't want to
burden them too. If I do tell them, they will feel they have
to do something, and I don't think anything can be done."

BREAKING SILENT AGREEMENTS

Communication is the key to breaking the silent agreements. If a family is not communicating with one another,

relationships will continue to erode. You and the other members of your family must begin talking. Just as important, you need to put aside blame and fear and *listen* to one another. This sounds easy enough, right? But it is not so easy. Most likely, you will find many barriers in your way. As you already know, change isn't free of conflict.

It is not in your power as a family to make the mental illness vanish. However, you do have the power to change how you cope, interact, and react. The first step is to talk openly with each other about silent agreements, decisions regarding the mentally ill person, feelings, concerns, and what each member wants and needs from the family.

Too often when you do try to talk to others in your family the response is disappointing. Family members may become angry or defensive and refuse to talk further when you bring up subjects that have always been "taboo." The more openly you express your feelings, the more defensive they may become. They may not be receptive to your ideas about changing family interactions or bringing secrets out in the open.

It's tempting to conclude that they are just not good listeners, and that any dialogue is impossible. But perhaps there is more to it. Often it is not *what* you say that upsets them but *how* you say it. There are many styles of communication that can alienate others. Listen to your next conversation with someone close to you, and try to notice whether any of your comments could be interpreted as accusing, threatening, ridiculing, belittling, ignoring, blaming, or discounting that person. For example: *"You don't* care about the family. Since you've left, *you're not involved* with us anymore. You only call during the holidays. *Why do you even bother to call at all?*" These remarks are filled with blame and accusations. The same concerns and feelings can be expressed more honestly: *"I feel* angry and hurt about you being gone so much. Even though I *want* to see you, *I get upset* because I only hear from you on holidays. Why is that, Vance? Why don't we hear from you more often?"

In the second example, Lynn is telling Vance how *she* feels, asking for what *she* wants, and checking things out for *herself.* In contrast, in the first example, Lynn is assuming a lot about Vance (that he doesn't care about the family), and she is not speaking for herself. She is not being open and honest with Vance about how she feels and what she wants; instead she is accusing him of bad behavior. Breaking the silence means being honest about how *you* feel and what *you* expect from others.

There is no need to break the silence the way a football player attempts to break through a defensive line. When you decide to break the silence, imagine a candle that pierces the darkness.

Be Like a Shammes

Be like a shammes for your family. The shammes is the candle that is used to light the other candles of the Menorah, the candelabrum used during the Hanukkah celebration. Among other things, the custom of lighting candles at Hanukkah symbolizes survival against all odds. Be a shammes. Bring light to the family by sharing your light, your insight, your love. Just as the shammes shares its flame but does not shed light for the other candles, your family can be a shammes to other families and these families a light for their communities.

As a shammes sheds light, it also casts a shadow. The brighter the light, the darker the shadow. Consequently, when you confront your family with an intent to "shed some light," remember to be sensitive to the shadows that will also reveal themselves.

When you tell your family that you are no longer willing to keep any silent agreements, that you won't hide how you feel or what you think, it may seem as if you are swimming upstream. You will be going against the direction of the river—your family's expectations and silent agreements. When you begin to swim upstream against the family's silence, it is usually denial, fear, and grief that you are swimming against. But keep swimming; the direction of the river is sure to change, or at the very least, you will reach the shore.

When the opportunity arises for you to talk with your family, approach them with an open mind. Try to leave bitterness outmoded expectations, or an unwillingness to compromise behind.

Communication: Your Bond to One Another

The family has an enormous amount of power and influence on people. It is the origin of most of one's personal dilemmas. But the family can also be a place where one is healed, a haven in which you give and receive love, acceptance, approval, and guidance. Ideally, the parents would be the ones to call the family together, open up conversations about feelings and decisions, and encourage family members to problem-solve together. However, when this does not happen, a sibling or adult child may, as a shammes, attempt to bring the family together.

Open up the communication between you and your family. Open communication means expressing your love and concern for each other in a more honest and direct fashion. It includes:

- Listening—being attentive to what others say
- Involvement—interest in what the other person is saying
- Respect—taking the other person's feelings seriously
- Honesty—a willingness to be open about your feelings and concerns

If you intend truly to communicate with someone, you have to become an active listener. Listening to others is a skill, especially when the conversation is an emotional one. Being a good listener means that your attention is not on what you plan to say next or on how you feel about what someone else is saying, but rather on what you actually hear him telling you. Next time you are in a conversation with someone, *just listen.*

Don't express your thoughts or feelings until it is your turn. When the person speaking is finished with what he has to say, repeat what you understood him to say. His response may be, "That's right, that's exactly what I mean," or he may have to clarify it for you because you didn't understand him. It's through active listening that you can better understand what the other person feels and thinks and arrive at a compromise.

Everyone knows how to talk, but not everyone can express his thoughts and feelings both tactfully and clearly. If, for example, you express anger by criticizing the other person, it is unlikely that the two of you will reach an agreement. Your criticism is likely to cause the other person to retreat. When you are the one talking, be specific about what you are trying to say. The more honest and direct you are about what you are thinking and feeling, the better your chances are of being understood. No one can read minds, although most people act as if that were possible.

FIGHTING FAIR

Once you get together and start making decisions, there is bound to be some conflict. Angry, hurt feelings are likely to arise and a fight may break out. But you and your family can survive conflicts. As long as they don't block open communication, arguments can even assist decision-making. You don't have to storm out of the house—you can stay and fight, as long as you *fight fair.*

When you discover yourself in the midst of an argument, consider the following guidelines for expressing your anger:

- As you start feeling angry, acknowledge these feelings with a simple statement like, "I feel angry about . . ."
- Accept that each member of the family has a right to his angry feelings. Try not to take someone else's feelings personally.
- Acknowledge that everyone is responsible for his own feelings of anger. Avoid such statements as *"You* make me

angry," or "*You* always do this to me."

- Do not start a family meeting or important discussion when someone is tired. Imaginative problem-solving is difficult if someone is tired.
- Do not belittle or make light of anyone's angry feelings.
- Deal with one issue at a time. Do not overload the argument with more than one concern.
- When you share your feelings be as specific as you can about what is upsetting you. State your concern in clear, objective terms: "I am angry that you went to visit John in the hospital instead of attending my volleyball game. This game meant a lot to me."
- Do not assume you know what others in the family are thinking or feeling until you ask.
- Do not tell others what they "should" feel or think.
- No name calling or put downs, since this will only cause others to get defensive or withdraw.
- Avoid sarcasm. Sarcasm is a way we cover up our true feelings of anger, sadness, or hurt. It also alienates others and sounds like a put down.
- Try not to bring up past mistakes, hurts, or grievances; talk about *present* issues and grievances only.
- Even though it may be embarrassing or painful, have the courage to admit when you are wrong. This encourages others in the family to do the same.

When the communication gets tense, think *compromise.* Try to avoid "right and wrong" formulations and focus on finding points of similarity and agreement, as Rhonda does in the following example:

"My mother accused me of being selfish when I told her I couldn't take my brother, Peter, for the week while she and Dad went on a vacation. Frankly, Peter and I never got along, and after he became sick our relationship worsened. I can't understand how my mother expects me to come home and baby-sit a twenty-seven-year-old! I finally asked

her why she feels he can't stay by himself for a week, and
she began to cry. She told me that he attempted suicide
twice in the last month and she fears for his life. She said, 'I
can't go on a vacation thinking Peter will kill himself while
I'm gone. I'm so afraid he's not going to live long enough
to get better.' I decided then that we should look for a solution that would work for both of us. I also told my mom
that we needed to talk more often."

Listening carefully to what the other person is really saying
will help make compromise possible.

Everyone lives with contradictions. In fact, within you are
many contradictory feelings: love and resentment; loyalty and
guilt; respect and jealousy; hope and fear. When arguments
occur you can assume that others in your family also experience complex, contradictory emotions and that they are
doing the best they can; they simply may not have developed
the skills and emotional resources to express themselves honestly and openly.

You can help turn every argument into a chance to *negotiate*. When you negotiate, make reasonable requests of others.
Asking for promises and guarantees is a way of setting yourself
up for disappointment. No one can honestly honor a guarantee. Instead, think about what is realistic in a given situation.
Some kind of resolution should be reached by those involved.
In some cases this means that you agree to disagree.

CALLING A FAMILY MEETING

The best response a family can have to a crisis, or a shift in
a family member's mental health, is to sit down and talk with
one another. Rather than making isolated decisions which
affect everyone in the family, make decisions as a team. The
purpose of a family meeting is to create a forum for the discussion of alternatives. The goal is to come up with a plan that
is acceptable to everyone. Sometimes the plan will be that the
family needs more time to generate alternatives.

Preparing for a family meeting takes some simple, logical steps so it can be a positive and safe experience for everyone. It should be planned ahead of time, and a minimum of three undisturbed hours should be set aside. The meeting should take place in one of the family member's homes, not in a public setting that might prove distracting. Children under the age of five should not be present since they will most likely demand attention from their parents. However, children five and older can attend if this is the parents' preference. It is important for everyone to show up on time and not to leave earlier than planned.

Because calling a family meeting will cause some tension, the purpose of the meeting should be explained in advance to every family member. The point is not to catch anyone off guard, so don't attend with a hidden agenda. Assuming you are the one asking for a meeting, contact all available family-members to ask them to attend; tell them what you want to discuss and the time and place.

Some families choose to have an objective person facilitate the meeting, such as a friend or a mental health professional; this again is up to the discretion of each family. Be sensitive to the other family members; some may feel more comfortable with a friend or professional acting as a "moderator," but others may not attend if an outsider is present. In addition, decide ahead of time whether or not to include in-laws. Since they are affected by the decisions made by their spouses, including them will strengthen your extended family and give them the opportunity to support their loved ones.

It may or may not be a good idea to invite the family member who is mentally ill to the family meeting. If he is hospitalized, hostile toward the family, or psychotic, it is probably not realistic to include him. In those cases, talk with him as soon after the family meeting as possible. Go over what was discussed and any decisions that were made. Since he will probably be expected to honor certain agreements, he should be given the opportunity to make requests or contribute his opinions. However, if the mentally ill family member is stable, he should be present and involved in the decision-making and any contract the family may write.

WRITTEN AGREEMENTS: YOUR FAMILY'S CONTRACT

At some point your family may want to draw up a family agreement that contains specific action plans. This clarifies everyone's expectations and responsibilities, making it easier for everyone to honor the solutions that are agreed upon.

The contract should include everyone in the family, including in-laws, and should contain specific steps and arrangements to deal with a given problem. It should cover both immediate problems and plans for the future. Ideally, the contract will assist the mentally ill person toward the greatest degree of autonomy possible. Before you sit down and write up a contract with your family, do an inventory of what you want covered in the agreement. Consider the following in your inventory:

- What has caused the most conflict within the family?
- What most needs to be written up and agreed upon?
- Who has been held responsible, up till now, for making the decisions?
- What are the silent agreements that need to be brought out into the open?
- What issues other than the mental illness need to be discussed?
- Who is expected to be responsible for the future care of the mentally ill person?
- How accountable is the mentally ill member to the family?
- How has the family decided to handle the likelihood of another crisis, such as a psychotic episode?
- How will the family respond to the mentally ill person refusing to take his medication?

Use the techniques for imaginative problem-solving described in Chapter 6 to come up with your written agreement. A contract will reduce the chaos and unpredictability that has been a part of your family relationships. It's not complicated; it can be as simple as the sample contract shown on the next page.

A copy could be given to each family member. It is likely that the terms or conditions of the agreement may need to be changed. Family meetings are a good place to go over the terms of the agreement and make any necessary changes.

KEEPING IT SIMPLE

A tradition in the twelve-step program for families of alcoholics is to *keep life simple*. For you this can mean dealing with one issue at a time. Don't weigh yourself down with worries, silent agreements, and problems. Keep your life simple. Do what you need to do to take care of yourself and the challenge at hand, and then let go of trying to make certain things happen. Once you communicate your feelings, hold a family meeting, or write a family contract, let go of it and get on with your life. Continue on your journey. In fact, you may want to write a written agreement for yourself. In this contract you could agree to take care of yourself, to work on the Eight Stage Healing Process described in Chapter 8, and to let go of problems by simplifying your life. Simplifying your life means freeing yourself from silent agreements. Secrets are extra baggage you don't need on your journey through life.

Be like a sea gull who travels across the vast ocean with a single twig in his mouth. At first you may think that the sea gull is foolish to carry a twig such a great distance only to build himself a home on the other shore. But notice that as the sea gull tires he places the twig on the water and rests. The twig is not only for his home on the distant shore; it is his place of rest as he travels. The sea gull's attention is on the *journey*, not his destination.

Keep it simple. Concentrate on doing what you need to continue your journey. This may be as simple as taking the time to rest along the way. It may mean saying "no" to someone. Pay attention to the journey, to the present moment and what you need now, and you will reach your destination.

SAMPLE FAMILY AGREEMENT

1. Everyone in the family has a right to speak about his feelings and concerns.

2. When we meet as a family to discuss issues, we will use guidelines for fair fighting.

3. We will hold Joseph accountable for his behavior. If he does something illegal or harmful, he will be expected to deal with the consequences. We will not rescue him from experiencing the consequences of his behavior.

4. During holidays we will focus on celebrating and leave discussing problems for another scheduled time.

5. If Joseph decides to go off his medication, he will be expected to move out of the house. He can only remain living with Mom and Dad as long as he remains on his medication.

6. Dad will go into the hospital for an evaluation of his drinking habits. As a family we will respect the hospital's assessment of whether or not Dad has a drinking problem.

7. In the event of a crisis, we will take the time to problem-solve as a family.

8. We will hold family meetings once a month.

We agree that the statements above are fair and agree to their conditions and terms. Signatures of all those involved:

_____   _____

_____   _____

Last night, as I was sleeping,
I dreamt —marvelous error!—
that I had a beehive here
inside my heart.
And the golden bees
were making white combs
and sweet honey
from my old failures.

- ANTONIO MACHADO

8

The Eight Stages

"But before I look out. . . Let me first gaze within myself"
— RAINER MARIA RILKE

"In a dark time, the eye begins to see."
— THEODORE ROETHKE

The Eight Stages offer you, the relative or friend of the mentally ill, a healing process through which to develop a new way of life. The stages are a tool to help you make positive changes in your relationships. Inevitably, the changes you undergo as you move through this process will foster healthier relationships not only with your mentally ill relative/friend, but with everyone else in your life. In fact, the Eight Stage Healing Process, although developed for families with mental illness, can be used for any troubled relationship. As in all personal growth programs, the ability to improve your life and relationships is dependent entirely on you—not on the expectation that the other person will recover from his dis-ease, be it alcoholism or mental illness.

What does it mean to be involved in a healing process, such as the Eight Stages? It enables you to identify what stands in the way of a satisfying life, to free yourself from the behaviors, attitudes, and relationships which keep you from expressing your full potential. It helps you to take the steps to improve your life and relationships. *Your happiness and peace of mind become a priority.*

Making your own happiness a priority isn't selfish. Our journey of becoming healthier and more satisfied with ourselves is not "self centered." We're not trying to get all the happiness and pleasure for ourselves. It's a process of developing compassion and a true understanding for others as well. By building our own strength and well-being we are in a better position to truly help other people.

The time and energy you put into your healing process will determine what you get out of it. Any healing process will take commitment and consistency. When the process gets difficult, it is important that you persevere. When you are feeling the most discomfort, it is because you are breaking negative habits. It means you are breaking the patterns that have kept you a Caretaker or Escape Artist. It means your relationships are taking new shape.

The Eight Stages guide you through stages of change. Each person will progress through the stages at his or her own pace and in his or her own way. When working on the Eight Stage Healing Process choose which relationships or issues you want to work on. Have a vision in mind of what changes you want to occur as a result of working with the Eight Stages. Do you want to improve family relationships? Exactly how do you want these relationships enhanced? What has kept you from intimacy and what are you willing to do to be in an intimate relationship? What do you hope to have accomplished after six months of working with the Eight Stages?

Just as you cannot bake an apple pie without apples, you need certain ingredients to make a program successful. In addition to the Eight Stages, your program needs to include the help of others. Join a group of people who are also working on the Eight Stage Healing Process. Therapists, mental health centers, local Alliance for the Mentally Ill affiliates, hospitals, and clinics across the country are beginning to offer the Eight Stages to their clients. If your area does not offer such a group refer to Chapter Nine: Reaching Out for Help, or the Resource Guide to the Eight Stages in the back of this book.

Begin by reading through the Eight Stages alone without doing the suggested work. Then, on the second reading, keep a journal and work on the stages with the strength and help of your group.

THE EIGHT STAGES
A Healing Process for the Families and Friends of the Mentally Ill

Stage One
AWARENESS. I explore the ways in which the relationship/ family has affected my life.

Stage Two
VALIDATION. I identify my feelings about this relationship and share those feelings with others.

Stage Three
ACCEPTANCE. I accept that I cannot control any other person's behavior and that I am ultimately responsible only for my own emotional well-being.

Stage Four
CHALLENGE. I examine my expectations of myself and others and make a commitment to challenge any negative expectations (silent agreements).

Stage Five
RELEASING GUILT. I recognize mental illness as a dis-ease and release the attitude of blame.

Stage Six
FORGIVENESS. I forgive myself for any mistakes I have made. I forgive and release those who have harmed me.

Stage Seven
SELF-ESTEEM. I return the focus of my life to myself by appreciating my own worth, despite what may be going on around me.

Stage Eight
GROWTH. I reaffirm my accomplishments and set daily, monthly, and yearly goals.

STAGE ONE
AWARENESS
I explore the ways in which the
relationship/family has affected my life.

This stage requires a willingness to take a personal inventory of your family relationships and the relationship with the mentally ill person, and to explore how both have influenced your life and other relationships.

It may be difficult to imagine that you would benefit from taking a personal inventory. After all, you are not the one who is mentally ill. Fear of blame can cause you to look everywhere but within yourself for answers. However, taking an inventory does not imply that you are doing something wrong. Rest assured that the very purpose of an inventory is to allay such fears. Through such an inventory you are more likely to realize that no one is to blame. If you harbor feelings of guilt, resentment, fear, hostility, or jealousy, take a look at *yourself*. A personal inventory then, is a search into your own mind and heart.

An inventory also includes a look at your past and present relationships. If you are unhappy with a relationship, it is time to focus on changing yourself instead of trying to get the other person to change. Many of your past attempts to change others were probably met with resistance and frustration. Through a better understanding of yourself, you can discover what it is in your power to change in a given relationship. In addition, such an investigation will reveal the healthy aspects of the relationship, and you'll be better able to strengthen them.

Too often, people in a relationship with a mentally ill person do not give themselves permission to focus on themselves. A personal inventory is a statement that you count, that it matters how you feel and react to a relationship. It begins the process of returning the focus of your life back to yourself.

As the thirty-seven-year-old son of a mentally ill father explains: "I didn't understand why I should take a personal inventory or work on the Eight Stages. I had a supply of reasons why it would be a waste of my time. I actually felt angry because I thought it wasn't me who had problems, it was my father who was sick. But then I started looking at how the relationship with my father had affected me. I'm the oldest of seven sons, but I'm the one who has always rushed our father to the hospital or searched for the best doctor. And he goes through doctors the way the rest of us go through socks. He always becomes suspicious of them and refuses to do what they suggest. I was also the one he abused the most when he became angry. He was never very kind or loving to any of us. But I always excused this because of his illness. I excuse everything—even my own loneliness. I've always believed that there is nothing I can do to change things—just as I could never change his sickness. Life seemed in someone else's control. I'm not at all sure what I'm going to do with these realizations. At age thirty-seven I think it is hard to change. But I want different things now—like a life of my own."

In Stage One you awaken to the knowledge that your problems are within you and your relationship to others. Within is also the ability to make all the positive changes you want. You begin to understand why you feel, behave, and think the way you do. Start by asking yourself how the relationship has influenced you. Use the following questions to begin your inventory:

- How would you describe the relationship to the person with mental illness?
- How would you describe your relationship to other family members?
- What was/is expected of you in your relationships?
- Are you honest about your feelings with the mentally ill person?

- Are any of your relationships abusive in any way?
- Did you excuse this person's abusive behavior? If so, how do you feel about this?
- How do you act around the mentally ill person?
- Are you concerned or preoccupied with the belief that you or your children may be mentally ill?
- What fears do you have in response to the mental illness?
- Are you concerned by what the future holds for you or your family?
- How have family relationships changed since the onset of the mental illness?
- What has the relationship to the mentally ill person taught you about your responsibility to others?
- How has the relationship with the mentally ill person affected how you feel and interact with other family members?

These are only a few sample questions to help you get started. You and your therapist or group may come up with different ones that are more specific to you. It is important that you describe in detail what this relationship was like for you, how it changed when the mental illness occurred, and what the relationship is like now. If your relative or friend committed suicide, identify the ways in which this loss has affected you. You are encouraged to write your inventory in a journal, since you may make use of it in future stages.

This stage ends the denial prevalent in so many families: that mental illness is a dis-ease that disrupts only the life of the afflicted person. Stage One helps you to explore the many ways the mental illness has affected you.

Your Personal Testimony

Each of us has a story to tell. This story is the story of what happened to us, our experiences, our perceptions, our history. Within our history is a mine full of precious jewels. In order to get to these jewels we have to dig through rock, dirt, ancient artifacts and debris. The tools needed to do the digging include the Eight Stages and getting help from an experienced "digger." The help will come through the form of an Eight Stage group and the experience can be from a therapist or trained facilitator.

Once you have these tools: the Eight Stages, a therapy/self-help group and a trained facilitator, you are ready to do some serious digging to get at those jewels. Those jewels include your self-esteem, goals, joy, creativity, and healthy relationships. Telling your story to others in a supportive group environment will be of immense benefit to you. You deserve to have others hear your story, to support you, to cry and laugh with you.

Giving a personal testimony is a powerful healing experience for everyone in the group. This most likely will be the first time you have shared your story in this way. Telling your story is another way to break through the silence that surrounds you and your family. Because you may likely be breaking silent agreements and telling some "family secrets," expect to feel uncomfortable. This is quite natural.

Marie became invisible at an early age. Being one child in six made it easy to hide when the problems in the family arose. Her father was an alcoholic, who sexually abused two of her sisters. One of her sisters was later diagnosed with manic-depression. Another one attempted suicide several times. Marie was sworn to secrecy. In fact, one sister who confronted her father around the abuse was shunned by the entire family. Marie went from this family into a severely abusive marriage, where she was punished any time she spoke up. She said she came into therapy when she was nearly dead inside. After a year of therapy she joined an Eight Stage group where she told her story for the first time. Before she began her story she said to the group "It's difficult being invisible when you have 2 hours to share your story."

Marie is no longer invisible.

Recommended reading with Stage One:

<u>Home Coming: Reclaiming and Championing Your Inner
    Child</u> by John Bradshaw; Bantam Books, 1990.

STAGE TWO
VALIDATION
I identify my feelings about this relationship
and share those feelings with others.

If you have denied that the mental illness and family relationships has had an effect on you, your feelings in response
to these relationships has also been denied. In this stage you
identify and express your many emotional reactions to the
mentally ill person and family relationships. You open yourself up to the myriad of emotions that you have contained
inside you, many which will lead you to the buried jewels.
Repressed feelings of anger, fear, guilt, sadness, resentment,
and shame must be released.

You may have wondered if your feelings are justified, or
whether others have similar feelings. Chances are you have
not taken the opportunity to seek validation for these feelings.
The goal of this stage is to reassure you that you are not alone
and your feelings are valid. Stage Two allows you time to vent
these emotions and encourages you to seek out people who
will be accepting, sympathetic, and able to identify with many
of your emotions. Stage Two can be accomplished with trusted friends, with your therapist or your Eight Stage group.

Identify the many feelings you held in because of the
silence within the family. Identify and share the feelings you
have now about your memories, the present, and about your
future. If your relative or friend committed suicide or died
from other causes, this stage is a necessary prelude to recover-

ing from your loss.

Next, seek validation from others for these feelings. Validation can be found in your self-help group, with trusted peers, and with others with whom you have rapport. Psychotherapy can provide reinforcement but should not take the place of the support and validation one can receive only from peers. It is comforting and empowering to receive recognition from others who have similar feelings and relationships. Your feelings will be part of your personal testimony (Stage 1).

During this stage seek out those who offer hope and encouragement, and avoid those who support negative feelings, like guilt or fear. The object is to recognize and express your feelings, not to dwell on negative emotions. The purpose is to get to the jewels buried within you, this means allowing the emotions to arise as you "dig." The powerful healing effects of opening up to others who are confronting similar problems cannot be underestimated.

Recommended reading with Stage Two:

How to Survive the Loss of a Love
by Melba Colgrove, Ph.,D., Harold H. Bloomfield, M.D., & Peter McWilliams, Bantam Books, 1981.

STAGE THREE
ACCEPTANCE

I accept that I cannot control any other person's behavior and that I am ultimately responsible only for my own emotional well-being.

Many of us learn to become responsible for someone else's

life and *emotional well-being*. Caretaking then not only involves the daily or medical needs of the mentally ill person but also a responsibility for his emotional well-being. When your loved one is feeling sad, you may feel sad. When he feels anxious, you feel anxious. In time, you may find it increasingly difficult to separate yourself from your mentally ill loved one. Perhaps you are unable to give yourself permission to enjoy yourself when a family member is upset.

Unfortunately, you are more likely to be manipulated into meeting the requests of others if you feel responsible for their emotional well-being. They only have to say they are hurt, upset, or angry and you will devote your energy to making them feel better. Accustomed to your intervention, they may eventually begin blaming you for how they feel. That is when you must insist that you are responsible only for your own emotional well-being.

Begin by repeating aloud to others in your group the following two statements:

"I accept that I cannot control any other person's behavior."
"I accept that I am responsible only for my own emotional well-being."

What are your thoughts and feelings after repeating these statements? Are you saying to yourself, "I must take care of him; after all, he's mentally ill?" Or perhaps you feel guilty. You may feel so strongly that you are responsible for someone else that you refuse to repeat these statements. The truth is you are not able to control anyone's behavior unless *he chooses to let you*. You cannot influence the emotional well-being of another person without his consent. And you cannot force someone to consent to be happy.

Now think back to times you have tried to control others' behavior. Think about how you felt when their behavior did not meet your expectations. No matter how disabled or ill another person is, you are not responsible for his behavior. This does not mean that you are not loving and respectful. It is the releasing of control that allows you to separate your needs from those of the other person and allows him to grow, fail, and change at his own pace. If you try to control another, you get caught up emotionally in what you believe to be the way he *should* behave. You become more involved in watching someone else's behavior in a given situation than in directing your own. You are then attempting to play God.

Some people derive pleasure and self-esteem from the belief that they are a benevolent and powerful presence in the life of their mentally ill relative. But it is a false sense of self-esteem. Consequently, these people become dependent on the mentally ill person's appreciation or improvement. Unfortunately, the mentally ill relative/friend rarely demonstrates this improvement or appreciation to a degree that satisfies the Caretaker. If your goal is to experience satisfying, loving relationships, you must stop taking the responsibility for others' lives and start taking full responsibility for your own. Although extreme, family members can become so invested in the mentally ill person's life that life *without* such a problem would feel empty.

If you want to effect positive change in the life of your mentally ill relative, *set an example,* but stop attempting to control his behavior or emotional state.

Recommended reading for Stage Three:

<u>The Language of Letting Go: Daily Meditations for Codependents</u> by Melody Beattie, A Hazelden Book/ Harper Collins; 1990.

STAGE FOUR
CHALLENGE
I examine my expectations of myself and others and make a commitment to challenge any negative expectations (silent agreements).

Beliefs and expectations are most often reinforced by our families. For example, your family may believe that your mentally ill family member's drinking and marijuana smoking are helping him cope with his mental illness. Or your parents may expect that your ill relative will live with you when they can no longer provide for him. In this stage you identify and examine your family's beliefs, expectations, and *silent agreements*. Because they vary from family to family, it is an inventory only you can take.

Your home was your classroom, teaching you how to deal with conflict, develop relationships, and respond to the expectations of others. Beliefs are what dictate our habits. Because our unhealthy beliefs and negative assumptions cause unhealthy behaviors, it is important to challenge them. Negative beliefs and expectations that go unchallenged will remain a part of your personal makeup and will affect all your relationships. What beliefs and silent agreements are you acting out that are self-defeating?

Consider the silent agreements and expectations Holly shares with her parents: Holly has a younger brother, Cecil, who is manic-depressive. Her parents have allowed Cecil to live with them. He is not expected to attend any treatment programs, since they believe that he "is too intelligent for those programs, and besides they won't accept him anyway." Holly is unable to suggest alternatives for Cecil to her parents because they have taken charge of Cecil's affairs. Holly *assumes* (silently agrees) that she will take over for her parents when they can no longer care for Cecil. She feels that if she were not to care of Cecil, she would be irresponsible. Although she shares some of the responsibility involved with the care for her brother, she frequently feels resentful and afraid of what her future holds.

Holly silently agrees with her parents on the expectation that she will be Cecil's future primary caretaker, but she is also resentful about it since these expectations directly affect her plans for the future. They also interfere with how she interacts and feels toward her parents and Cecil. Consequently, she feels torn between her feelings of loyalty and guilt.

Each family member is valuable. *If a family's way of dealing with mental illness is not in the best interest of all its members, then it is not the best solution.* It is up to Holly, and each of us, to challenge any negative beliefs and expectations (silent agreements) generated within our families. If the expectation or solution directly affects your future, you would do well to make sure it is a healthy one.

When you challenge your family's way of coping, they may be resistant. Be prepared! Get support from those in your Eight Stage group. Remember, you are laying the groundwork for all the relationships in your life. Don't let others' beliefs and expectations steer your life, and don't cling to beliefs and expectations that are self-defeating. Be the captain of your ship, identify all family rules and expectations, and challenge those which are negative or harmful.

Begin by asking yourself if you are happy with the present outlook of your life. Many people assume that beliefs and expectations cannot be changed, and say to themselves, "This is how things are." "This is what I *should* do as a sibling/child/parent/friend." "I can't come up with any other ways to handle my problems." "I would be a bad person if I did things differently." However, beliefs *can* change. A good place to start is with all the "musts" and "shoulds" that are a sign of the silent agreements by which you are living. Ask yourself where these "musts" and "shoulds" came from and why they are such strong convictions. Then, think of yourself as in a phase of renewal. Begin again by investigating your present beliefs, challenging them, changing those that are unhealthy, and keeping those that are life-enhancing.

When you are ready to further challenge those beliefs, write out, preferably in your journal, answers to the following questions:

What do others expect of me in relation to my mentally ill family member?

What are some shared beliefs within my family about my brother, sister, child, or parent's mental illness?

What do I believe is the cause of the mental illness? How does this affect how I interact with my family and how does it affect the plans I make for our futures?

What do I believe would help my mentally ill family member get well?

At this time, what is my biggest fear?

After you answer these questions, review what you have written. Then challenge these beliefs and assumptions by asking *"Why?"* for each answer you have written. For example:

Why do your parents believe that your sibling with mental illness shouldn't be held accountable when he threatens you?

Why does your family tolerate a member's erratic and bizarre behaviors?

Why does your family expect you to be the one to admit your mentally ill mother into the hospital each time she becomes psychotic?

Why do you share the belief that mentally ill people are not responsible for their behavior?

Why do you share the belief that all the behaviors of your relative/friend are the direct result of the mental illness?

Why do you believe the cause of the mental illness is drugs?

Why do you fear that you, too, may become mentally ill?

Why do you believe that the only thing that could help your mentally ill family member is a better mental health system?

Why do you fear that your parent or sibling will never be able to care for himself or herself?

It is best to write out the responses to these questions so they can be clearly understood and challenged.

Also take the time to identify the silent agreements you have with every family member. Don't leave anyone out. What silent agreements do you have with your parents/spouse/children/siblings?

The final step in this stage is to identify how these beliefs affect your feelings, goals, and relationships. How, for example, does the silent agreement that mentally ill people are never accountable for their behavior affect your life? How do you interact with the mentally ill person, and what do you and others expect of the person with mental illness? How do your fears affect your feelings and actions? How do any of your family's expectations affect you?

After you have completed these steps, you are in a position to decide which beliefs you will continue to hold and which you are ready to change.

Recommended reading with Stage Four:

Care of the Soul: A Guide for Cultivating Depth and Sacredness in Everyday Life by Thomas Moore., Harper Collins, 1992

STAGE FIVE
RELEASING GUILT
I recognize mental illness as a dis-ease and release the attitude of blame.

In this stage you confront the misconception that someone or something has to be *blamed* for the mental illness. You also confront the misconception that anyone else is responsible for *your* unhappiness. This stage is the natural continuation of stages Three and Four in which you recognize that you cannot control others' behaviors, and then release your feelings of over-responsibility for others.

Taking the responsibility for understanding your role in a given relationship does not mean you are to blame for anyone else's troubles. Families of the mentally ill often confuse being responsible for oneself with blaming oneself.

> "My husband was different right from the start. But I didn't think his 'differences' were signs that he had manic-depression. I was not prepared for the bouts of paranoia that immobilized him. For ten years I refused to take a look at our relationship, to believe that there was anything I could do. He got sicker and sicker and I got more and more frightened. I felt as if I had something to do with causing this horrible sickness that was taking my husband from me. I couldn't blame him because he was so unhappy—there was only me left to blame. Perhaps I wasn't a very good wife, I thought. Then one day a therapist asked me over and over again how I felt. When I finally said scared and angry she asked me what I was scared and angry about. I thought, 'What a stupid question, what is she getting at, anyway?' I reminded her that I was there to figure out what I could do to help my *family.* I was also afraid that my therapist would discover all the awful things I did as a mother and wife. It seems what I was most scared of was others discovering what I had done wrong."

Being responsible enough to take a look inward does not mean you were or are wrong. Blaming yourself or others won't change what happened. When a valuable piece of china breaks, you may be able to salvage a part of it, but you can't change the fact that it is broken. What's broken will never be what it once was.

This stage encourages you to *stop searching for the cause of the problem or the guilty party, and instead look for solutions for yourself in the present.* Again, the problem is no longer the mental illness, but how you have handled your life since the onset of the dis-ease.

As is the case for the majority of dis-eases and illnesses today, the causes and cures of mental illness are varied or unknown. There is a strong belief among family members that if they can only figure out the cause, everything will be all right. However, no matter what the cause, you cannot change the past or guarantee a cure. Whatever the cause, the family still needs to recover from the pain and disruption mental illness has caused *each* member. When you stop blaming yourself and others you will be able to accept what cannot be changed and change what you can.

Unfortunately, people often search obsessively for the cause of the mental illness or blame the mental health system rather than concentrating on the healing that needs to take place *within* themselves and their families. *It does not matter* if the cause was genetic or environmental. *It does not matter* if family problems, virus, or stress are suspected to be the cause. The solutions to your family's problems do not lie in searching for the cause. Leave this up to physicians and brain researchers. You are not directly responsible for the mental illness and you cannot control or cure it.

Even when family abuse is a contributing factor in the mental illness, blaming only keeps you stuck. You stay stuck in your feelings of shame and blame, rather than focus on what needs to heal. Blaming can distract us from finding solutions to our problems. Blame is usually a result of us projecting our feelings of shame onto others. Parent's feel shame, so they may blame the mental health system; sibling's feel shame so they may blame their parents. You can hold others accountable for their past and present behaviors without blaming. Are you blaming anyone else for *your* unhappiness? If you are, then the possibility of recovering your happiness is in their power, not yours. Claim responsibility for your own unhappiness, then you can do what it takes to feel better.

To help you let go of blame repeat the following statements:

"I didn't cause the illness."
"I can't control it and I can't cure it."

If you have trouble accepting these statements, challenge your beliefs and expectations as you did in Stage Four. For example if you believe you can control the illness, how can you do this? How can you cure the person of the dis-ease? How is this in your power? How did you cause the mental illness and why do you believe you caused it?

Also ask yourself who you are blaming for your unhappiness or problems? Even if you are in an abusive relationship blaming your partner only keeps you suck in the relationship. *Name the problem,* then take responsibility for your own safety and happiness. Blaming your partner won't change a thing.

There are two other steps you can take to affirm that you can't control the mental illness and that you can't cure it. These steps are valuable in helping you recognize that you are doing everything in your power to help others while looking after your own needs.

* Identify at least five positive gestures you have made toward your mentally ill relative or friend.
* Identify at least five behaviors you approve of or enjoy in your mentally ill loved one.

Once you have identified five behaviors you favor, begin to focus on them instead of the behaviors you dislike. This is an active practice of compassion—bringing to mind what you appreciate about the other person.

Recommended reading with Stage Five:

How Can I Help? by Ram Dass and Paul Gorman., Alfred A. Knoff, 1985

STAGE SIX
FORGIVENESS
I forgive myself for any mistakes I have made. I forgive and release those who have harmed me.

You can find freedom in forgiving your mentally ill loved one for not being the person you wish him to be. Forgiveness is the ability to release resentment, anger, and old hurts so that they no longer clutter your mind and weigh down your relationships. To practice forgiveness means to make an effort to release negative thoughts about yourself and others, and instead foster positive beliefs. It allows you to recognize that no one is perfect and allows others to grow at their own pace.

An original meaning of forgive meant to "give for," to give up. Here you give up thoughts that keep you resentful and angry. Forgiveness does not mean you condone the actions of the other, nor does it require you to associate with that person. To forgive someone does not guarantee that you will *forget* your past, but feelings of anger and resentment can diminish.

RELEASING EMOTIONAL PAIN

Emotional pain is analogous to physical pain. Suppose you had an accident last year in which you broke your leg. Perhaps you can remember how painful it was for you but you are also aware that it is no longer painful. Likewise, if your mentally ill relative has disappointed you, lied to you, frightened you, or harmed you in some way, you can choose to remember your hurt, but this need not lead to an unforgiving attitude. Being aware of your feelings of anger does not mean harboring resentment. While you need to express your anger, hurt, and fear, you also need to release it and forgive others for the harm they may have caused you. Forgiveness is not a self-righteous act but a powerful way of releasing the negative hold others or situations may have on you. Forgiveness is the ultimate act of love.

There are many ways to practice forgiveness. Some practice forgiveness through prayer and meditation, others through creative visualization and affirmations. Experiment until you find the technique that best suits you.

Here are two exercises in forgiveness you can use; the first one is about forgiving others and the second is about forgiving yourself. This may be read aloud to you by a friend or quietly to yourself. A trained group facilitator/therapist may also guide your group through these.

To practice forgiveness, find a quiet, safe place in which to be alone for approximately half an hour. (Unless you are doing it in a group setting.) Sit in a comfortable position and relax. If you have a favorite relaxation technique, use it. Otherwise, a simple technique is to close your eyes, inhale through your nose, hold your breath to the count of four, and exhale slowly through your mouth, sighing. As you exhale, let your body relax. Repeat this three times and then begin the first exercise.

Forgiving Others

With your eyes closed, imagine before you, the person you are forgiving. Conjure up as vivid a picture of this person as possible. You may have a certain incident in mind for which you are forgiving this person. Imagine telling this person how you would have preferred that he behave. Recall your feelings and thoughts. Recall all that you wished the person had or had not done.

For example, a daughter might imagine saying to her mother, "I would have preferred that you not go into the hospital again at Christmas. I wanted you to be a part of the holidays, without causing disruption and without leaving me alone with Dad and the boys. Instead you went into the hospital when I felt I needed you the most. You disappointed me. I wish you had stayed at home."

Notice how you are feeling as you deliver your imaginary speech. Repeat this part of the exercise until you reawaken the feelings you actually had in the past. Continue to remain in a relaxed state with your eyes closed. Stay with the feelings.

Now say something like this to the person: *"This is what I preferred, but you were unable or unwilling to do this. This does not change my wish that you would have acted differently. However, I now release you. I forgive you for not being able to do what I wished. I fully and freely release you. I no longer hold a grudge, nor am I angry with you for this. I forgive you. I am free of the harm you caused me. I let you go."* Continue saying this or similar phrases until you are satisfied that you believe what you are saying. Return yourself to the present and open your eyes.

When you *desire* to forgive, when you want to release the negative feelings, you will succeed at forgiving. Having once forgiven someone, you will have no need to forgive the person for the same incident again. This is the power of true forgiveness; it is unnecessary to repeat the exercise.

However, because you have been carrying negative, hurtful, or vengeful thoughts around with you for so long, they are likely to reappear. Whenever the person or the hurtful situation comes to mind, release him and say to yourself any of the following statements: "Peace be with you." "I have forgiven you." "This situation is in the past and no longer affects me." "I am free of the harm you caused me." After a time, the recollection of that particular experience will return less and less frequently until it is hardly remembered. Imagine that you are simply replacing a tape that plays in your head. The repeated statements of forgiveness and release are like a new recording.

Forgiving others does not say that the person who caused you harm should not be punished or reprimanded. It does not mean you do not hold him accountable for his harmful behavior. It *does* mean you do not carry with you the "harm" inside your body, mind and spirit. It *does* mean you come to truly understand that *someone elses' harmful behaviors are not about you.* You can be free of the harm. Forgiving others does not mean you are giving the person permission to repeat the offense. Even though you have forgiven someone does not mean you like the person or will choose to be with them.

Forgiving Yourself

This exercise uses a technique similar to the one above. Start by sitting in a relaxed position and practicing your chosen form of relaxation. Have a pen and paper handy. Close your eyes and remember to breath.

Imagine yourself as a child with a "larger you," a guardian, ready to speak to you from some point suspended in the air before you. The guardian is loving, supportive, forgiving, protective and advice-giving. The guardian is never critical. You trust your guardian completely. It is the part of you that understands how the child in you feels scared and hurt and that has the wisdom and insight to help you out. The Guardian accepts you *unconditionally*.

Now tell the guardian whatever has made you feel guilty or ashamed. For example, if you once abused yourself by drinking heavily or were cruel to someone you cared for, tell your guardian about it.

Throughout the exercise, don't forget to breath.

When you have finished telling the guardian about the incident, ask the guardian for forgiveness and guidance. Then sit back and listen to what the guardian has to say.

The guardian, in its insight, wisdom, and unconditional love for you, will help. You need to receive the message and forgiveness openly. Imagine yourself as a child listening to a loving parent, the parent within *you*. Trust what you hear.

After you have received the complete message, begin returning yourself to the present, to the room. Thank the guardian for the advice. Take three deep breaths and stretch. Count from five to one, and on the count of one open your eyes. Immediately record in your journal the suggestions or thoughts you received from your guardian.

The guardian within you will always forgive you. This is simply the exercise in which you take time to listen to your inner source of love, compassion and forgiveness. You have the power to free yourself from guilt, anger, and bitterness. Keep the message and refer to it in any future meditations if you wish.

As in the first exercise, if you begin to feel that you are judging yourself harshly again, repeat one of the following affirmations: "I have forgiven myself." "That is in the past; it is over." You can also repeat any of the messages your guardian gave to you.

Finally, remember to be patient with yourself. Patience is a form of self-forgiveness because you are acknowledging that you are limited as to how fast you can change. Do not expect to purge yourself of all guilt and shame in just a few days. Accept yourself as you are *now*. Allow yourself to make mistakes as you gradually change. Be kind to yourself.

Recommended reading with Stage Six:

The Wisdom of No Escape and the Path of Loving-Kindness by Pema Chŏdrŏn, Shambhala Publications, 1991.

STAGE SEVEN
SELF ESTEEM
I return the focus of my life to myself and appreciate my own worth, despite what may be going on around me.

Perhaps it has become a conditioned response to drop everything in order to take care of someone else or clean up after someone else's personal disaster. This would be true if you were a Caretaker. Perhaps it has become a conditioned response to avoid being involved with others while at the same time ignoring your own needs. This would be true if you were an Escape Artist. Both Caretakers and Escape Artists have learned to devalue their own needs.

Perhaps you do not value yourself because the focus of others' love and attention was on someone else for so long. If you have a family member with mental illness it is possible you were criticized by him in a way that further diminished your self-esteem. One purpose of Stage Seven is to help you appreciate yourself so that you are in a better position to extend love and caring to others. In addition, Stage Seven can help you remain centered and focused even when life is chaotic.

There will always be chaos and problems in life. It is not helpful to yourself or others to be easily controlled by outside circumstances and other people's problems. We are either part of the problem or part of the solution. When we get caught up in the drama and chaos of someone else's situation, we become part of the problem. This only adds to the stress in our own lives. Learn to stay centered—focused on your own worth despite chaotic cirmcumstances and you will find lasting happiness. As offered in Chapter 6, pages 119-121, *mindfulness meditation* is one of the most effective methods of teaching oneself such centeredness.

Do not put yourself second or feel unimportant because you assume you are not in as much need as the person with mental illness. Stop escaping from intimacy and learn to love yourself, so that others can love you.

BUILDING AFFIRMATIONS

You are now ready to learn techniques to help you change the negative beliefs you identified in Stage Four, Challenge. Described here is one technique of using affirmations to bring about positive change in oneself.

Affirmations are positive statements about yourself that you wish to make true. To affirm means to "make firm." You "make firm" what you desire by stating your desire as if it were already true. The practice of repeating affirmations will help you replace any outdated or destructive thoughts with positive ideas and thoughts. You may want to refer to your journal for negative self-concepts you identified in Stage Four.

The next step is to change these negative concepts about yourself to affirmations. All affirmations are:

- Written or stated in the first person
- Stated in positive terms (without using any negative references)
- Stated in the present tense (as if already true)
- Generally short and specific
- Supportive and encouraging
- Stated in your own words
- Designed to identify and validate what is true for you
- Stated without doubt or hesitation, reflecting your innermost desire for self-appreciation

Using these guidelines, take each negative statement and transform it into a positive statement about yourself and your experiences.

WEAK AFFIRMATION: It is *not* true that I am *selfish*.
STRONG AFFIRMATION: I *am* a loving person and I take good care of myself.

Finally, it is important to repeat your affirmations throughout the day, for a minimum of three weeks, or until you have a stronger sense that they are feeling true. You can read, think, say aloud, or even sing your affirmations. State your affirmations any time you catch yourself dwelling on any of the negative self-concepts you have identified. Many people find that the best times to state their affirmations are first thing in the morning (perhaps after your morning mediation) and immediately before going to sleep.

Your "mental diet" includes your affirmations, the material you read, the television programs you watch, and even your conversation with others. Choosing to repeat affirmations, reading self-awareness books, and engaging in satisfying relationships will help you have a more positive view of yourself and others.

Recommended reading with Stage Seven:

Creative Visualization by, Shakti Gawain., Whatever Publishing, 1978.

STAGE EIGHT
GROWTH
I reaffirm my accomplishments and set daily, monthly, and yearly goals.

Because the failures and successes of your mentally ill relative can have a profound influence on you, you are probably very attuned to his progress. In the meantime, you may have lost track of your own dreams and plans. Both Caretakers and Escape Artists have trouble setting goals. Rather than drifting through life, responding to a series of crises, you can be decisive about what you want to do and be.

Setting goals fuels the affirmations you designed in Stage Seven. Stage Eight completes the process of returning the focus of your life to yourself. You take the time and make the commitment to put your desires into skillful action. Perhaps you have never taken time before to set goals for yourself. Yet, you are clearly a person who can set goals for yourself because you have taken the time to work on the first seven stages.

The purpose of this stage is to help you recognize your achievements, overcome the obstacles that may be preventing you from setting personal goals, and learn to take action on your goals. To work on this stage, start by writing out a "wish list." Without judging your desires, include on the list *everything* you want or hope for. There are no right or wrong wants. This list can cover such areas as personal relationships, career, social life, possessions, feelings, spirituality, and family.

After you have written your list, use a colored pen to circle the goals you feel you most *want* to achieve. Then, with a pen of a different color, circle the goals you feel you are most *likely* to achieve. For example, you may have written that you wish to own a chain of hotels and that you wish to attend business school. Which of these wishes is more realistic? Circle it in the second color. In the coming years, your opportunities will increase as you attain more of your goals.

Now take all the wishes circled in the first color and put them on their own list entitled "Most Important Goals." Write a second list made up of those circled in the second color entitled "Possible Now."

Some wants will have been identified as both "most important" and "possible now." Draw up a third list of those you circled with both colors entitled "Want List." It's a good idea to keep all these wishes in your journal to refer to later.

The next step is to review your lists. Are your daily activities moving you toward or away from what you want? Are your relationships helping or blocking movement toward these wishes? Your Want List is made up of what you have identified as most important and most possible to accomplish. Are you at all close to fulfilling these wishes? It is time to transform your *wishes* into *goals*.

Goals are wishes fueled by motivation and determination to make them come true. Goals demonstrate that you care about yourself enough to tend to your own needs and future.

FOUR EASY STEPS TO GOAL SETTING

1. Make sure that you set realistic goals. If you set too many goals, you may feel overwhelmed and you are less likely to make progress toward any of them. That is why you have already narrowed it down by screening your personal Want List. You are now left with those wants which are most desired and most realistic.

2. Take the *Want List* and title it *"My Goals."* Then briefly

write out the benefits you will achieve from accomplishing each goal.

3. Assess how close you are to each of these goals. What do you need to accomplish before you have achieved each goal? Identify the specific steps you will take to achieve each goal. For example, if one of your goals is to attend college, you may first have to apply for a grant.

4. Next, make each step *measurable* by establishing a deadline for it. Remember, it takes a lot of little steps and commitments to achieve a greater goal. Having deadlines makes it possible to reward yourself when the steps to achieving your greater goal have been completed.

Dedicate time every morning to reviewing your goals. You may choose to write out a list of priorities of what needs to be accomplished. What is the most valuable use of your time today? If you had to leave town for a month, what would you have to finish before leaving? Give that your full attention. Concentrate on one thing until it is complete. Finally, relax and enjoy yourself after you have reached the goal you set out to achieve.

Skillful Action

Skillful refers to the *way we act out* our wishes and thoughts. The intent is to be as skillful as we can when taking action on our desires and goals. We realize just as other's behaviors have an effect on us, what we choose to do or not do, has impact on those around us.

Recommended reading with Stage Eight:

The Artist's Way: A Spiritual Path to Higher Creativity
by Julia Cameron., Putman Publishing Group, 1992

HEALING IS AN ONGOING PROCESS

The Eight Stages is an ongoing process. Sometimes you will find it helpful to return to a certain stage during a difficult time. We are never finished with a our healing process. Such a process is a way of life. Every day is the day to practice loving yourself. Every day is the day to practice reaching out for support and help. Every day is the day to repeat your affirmations. Every day is precious. When we come across obstacles on our journey we have the power to transform these into challenges and opportunities. We are able to do this not because circumstances have changed but because *we* have changed. As His Holiness the Dalai Lama said, *"Difficult experiences are very good training for the mind. They help us develop a kind of inner determination."*

When you get weary or discouraged remember to be kind to yourself. Be patient. But don't give up. Don't give up. Don't give up.

"On with it, then, and finish the job! Be as eager to finish it as you were to begin it, and do it with what you now have." II Corinthians 8:11

9

Reaching Out
for Help

Taking care of yourself does not mean "doing it all alone."
— SHAKTI GAWAIN

"A teacher or a culture doesn't create a human being. It doesn't implant within him the ability to love, or to be curious, or to philosophize, or to symbolize, or to be creative. Rather, it permits or fosters or encourages or helps what exists in embryo to become real and actual."
— MASLOW

Families of the mentally ill need groups where they can openly express their feelings, share concerns, exchange ideas, and find hope. They need a place they can safely break through the silent agreements—a place where they can open up and freely tell their many stories.

You Can't Heal In Isolation

The healing begins when you begin to speak to others about your feelings and thoughts. When you open up the the love and help that is available to you. For such healing to take place you need a group that is focused on *your* needs not on the needs of the mentally ill. This does not mean that the mental illness or the mentally ill relative will not be discussed.

Cynthia came to her first sibling group to get help for her sister. She listened to the introductions and the explanation of the group's purpose without asking any questions. She later commented that she found it difficult to accept that this group wasn't going to teach her how to help her sister. Rather, it was a group to support her. She felt both nervous and relieved.

"The moment I met the other group members I knew I had found home. Finally, I could talk about the pain I've had all these years about my father's mental illness. By the time we got through the introductions and the therapists explained the purpose of the group I was in tears. I've never cried in front of others before but my tears could not be contained. I was home."

"My therapist kept telling me, *Tamara, you can't heal in isolation,* reach out, join a group.' Then she finally started an Eight Stage group and I decided to take the risk and join it. I've been part of this group for two years and now I understand what she meant—we can't heal in isolation. We need each other."

Groups, lead at first by an trained lay-facilitator or therapist, provide a setting in which you can confront your fears, receive validation, experience positive relationships, and come to understand how the mental illness affects you. These groups can also offer examples of healthy ways to interact with your mentally ill relative and other family members. Participants often urge each other to "let go" of matters outside their control and begin focusing on themselves. As family members, you can make a conscious effort to practice caregiving skills with the support of the group and facilitator.

Ideally, these groups are facilitated by trained facilitators or therapists. Having a professional facilitate the group, at least at the onset, is an important component to establishing a healthy, safe group environment. Too many support groups repeat the many "coping" patterns found within the family structure, such as focusing on the needs/issues of the mentally ill. Too often what support groups *support* is negative coping patterns.

The purpose of a support group is to encourage healthy, life-enhancing behavior. Unfortunately, some groups may foster coping skills which are not necessarily healthy. Groups that engage in fault-finding or neglect problem-solving can be harmful. On the other hand, groups that encourage participants to help themselves and reinforce positive habits will enhance the participants' lives. If you are searching for a group, try and find one lead by a trained or professional facilitator. If you are joining up with a self-help group, *listen* to what is being said. Is the group focusing on the mentally ill person, negativity, and the cause of the illness, or is it focusing on family members, problem-solving, and solutions? Does the group feel safe to you?

Determining the Safety of the Group

One of the roles of a trained or professional facilitator is to assure the safety of the group for its members. They make certain you can open up with your story, your feelings and your many opinions without being harmed or hindered in any way. They can provide safe and healthy ways for conflicts to be expressed and resolved among group members.

To locate a local Eight Stage group, contact the local mental health clinic, or contact the Eight Stage's resource center, and refer to the back of this book for number and address. If you discover there are no groups available in your area, you have several options:

- Begin working on the Eight Stages with a therapist.
- Write a letter or call your local mental health clinic and request they offer such a group (several already do).
- After you have worked through the Stages at least once with a therapist, consider being trained as a facilitator yourself and begin your own group (refer to back of book).
- Ask your therapist to offer a group.
- Start a self-help group (guidance on this below).

Starting Your Own Eight Stage Group

Every community is home to a surprising number of families with mental illness. At one time or another all family members can benefit from attending an Eight Stage group. Whereas many choose not to do so, there are those who will be greatly relieved to discover your group. By publicizing its existence, you will reach families who may otherwise not know that such support exists. Hear are a few suggestions for announcing your group to the community:

- Arrange for an announcement in the newsletter published by the local Mental Health Association and Alliance for the Mentally Ill.
- Contact your local information and referral services through your city, county or state.
- Contact the community mental health clinics in your area.
- Submit a public service announcement to your local newspaper and radio stations.
- Place articles, letters, or announcements in the smaller neighborhood papers.
- Print flyers to post in the community.

Once you start your group, you may find that many participants drift in for only a couple of meetings. They may benefit from their experience but still not return. Groups with many "transient" members tend to be less cohesive. Realize that it takes great courage for many to attend their first meeting. Attending a gathering of people who are strangers, who meet to talk about an unpleasant topic, often causes fear and hesitancy. Typically, this is their first effort to share their personal stories with others.

How, then, can a group become cohesive, and how can group facilitators encourage regular participation? It is important that both facilitators and other members be sensitive to the fears of participants and that they work to create a nonthreatening atmosphere. It is also very important that the group's expectations are clear to all those who take part; an explanation of the group's purpose should occur at the beginning of each meeting. It is crucial that new members be welcomed. Introductions and a reading of the group guidelines (see p. 192) foster consistency and provide a time for questions. A commitment to attend a minimum of six to ten meetings allows time to develop relationships with other participants, creating a sense of responsibility and trust. Through consistent attendance, members not only receive support, but can return that support to others whom they have come to know in past meetings.

To further encourage attendance, structure sessions around the Eight Stages. After the eight sessions are completed, the participants can choose to continue if they wish.

YOUR MEETING PLACE

You can hold a group meeting in your home, a church, synagogue, or at your local mental health association or alliance for the mentally ill office, if there is one. Find a public place in a central and safe location. Religious institutions and local community colleges may donate a room for use as a meeting place. Some groups find it feasible to work in cooperation with a mental health clinic, which can provide space and professional support, and may help with publicity. It is preferable to hold meetings regularly at the same time and location. If you hold the group meetings in different locations each time it may create extra work, since each meeting is then organized separately by the facilitator.

CHOOSING A FOCUS FOR THE GROUP

Every self-help group has a purpose, ranging from helping people deal with addictions such as gambling to helping single mothers adapt to parenting. The more clearly defined the purpose, the more likely the group is to be successful at meeting the needs of its participants.

What is your group's purpose? What specifically do you hope to accomplish by forming a group for relatives of the mentally ill? Undoubtedly, family members attend for a variety of reasons—some are in crisis, while others need emotional support or referrals. Some individuals want counseling, while others are content to let off steam. One group cannot be everything to everybody. It will help both the facilitator and the participants to have a written statement of the group's purpose, which makes it clear who the group is designed for and what its purpose is. People interested in attending your Eight Stage group can review the statement and decide if it is appropriate for them. A statement of purpose might read like this:

We are a self-help group led by laypersons with mentally ill family members. We offer the the Eight Stage Healing Process as the focus of our work together. We sponsor monthly/weekly meetings. We do not promote any particular view of mental illness. Rather, we encourage the participation of all those seeking to improve their lives. We seek to create opportunities to discuss the issues that affect us and to draw upon one another's strengths, talents, and insights to effect positive change in our lives and the lives of our families.

This statement, along with the Eight stages can be read at the start of each group meeting.

Each group facilitator and member will bring his or her unique talents, style, and influence to the group. The following sample guidelines are not meant to be inflexible rules. Rather, they are provided to help you express your talents for the maximum advantage of the group. Facilitators who use guidelines find that leading meetings is a task which is not only manageable, but enjoyable.

The following guidelines are designed to encourage an atmosphere of support as well as furnish the group with leadership and a shared commitment. These guidelines may be read aloud at the beginning of meetings where there are new members. You may choose to type out these guidelines and have them available for group members.

SAMPLE GUIDELINES

- This is a self-help group for families of the mentally ill where we work on the Eight Stage Healing Process together.
- Each participant in this group is required to maintain confidentiality.
- This group is facilitated and participated in by families of the mentally ill.
- This group encourages an atmosphere of support, education, and self-improvement. Our group does not dictate any particular view of mental illness, and we give advice only when it is invited.
- This group is conducted in a respectful manner. We respect others' feelings, thoughts, and attitudes, and we do not expect everyone to share the same beliefs or opinions.
- This group encourages all members to participate at their

own pace; not everyone may be ready to share personal information.

- This group offers resources and literature about the Eight Stages, codependency, and family relationships.

Group meetings typically last two to three hours, with a ten-minute break at midpoint. A meeting should not, as a rule, last longer than three hours. It is up to the group leader for the evening to conclude the meeting at the time agreed.

BEING A GROUP FACILITATOR CAN BE FUN

Peer facilitators may wish to receive some leadership from professionals. Ideally you will receive some training on facilitation of an Eight Stage group. However, in no way do family members have to depend on professionals to sponsor such groups. The most valuable asset of a self-help group facilitator is his shared experience with group members. This "experience" includes having worked on the Eight Stages at least once with the help of a therapist. A peer group facilitator should not separate himself from the group, or adopt the role of a "therapist." Self-help groups are intended to provide a forum in which family members can learn to help themselves and each other.

A facilitator is like an orchestra leader; the group knows the tune, the facilitator just "conducts" the process. Several facilitators can alternate from meeting to meeting, or one can lead for a set period of time. Optimally, you will have a group of leaders who can share the responsibilities of conducting the group.

It is important to identify the facilitator for the evening at the start of each meeting. Then the participants can look to him for leadership and direction. It is up to the facilitator to ensure that everyone has a chance to talk. On an evening when participants are especially talkative this may be a challenge. Giving everyone a chance to speak requires assertiveness and may mean interrupting someone who is speaking.

One trick is to remind the group how much time is remaining and who else is left to speak. The following statements would help to keep people aware of time limits: "We have about twenty minutes. Who would like to talk next?"

Another skillful technique to keep the group on time is to designate how much time each member has to share at the beginning of the group . Then, when someone takes their time, they can ask for a "timer," to let them know when their time is up. This takes the pressure off the facilitator and allows the other members to help in keeping each other accountable to the time available.

Your own personal knowledge and experiences as the relative of a mentally ill person are your best skills in this group. Use them to support others in ways you would like to be supported and encourage productive, caregiving behavior and attitudes. As you read the seven basic skills of an effective self-help group facilitator listed below, ask yourself if you possess them.

- **Empathy**—demonstrating an understanding and appreciation of others' feelings. You extend support and comfort as others express their feelings, but do not feel compelled to rescue them from their hurt; instead you show them your concern.

- **Active Listening**—being attentive to what others are saying. You encourage others to share their thoughts without jumping in and giving unsolicited advice. When someone is speaking, you are attentive to what he is saying rather than to your emotional response to it. If you do not understand him, you ask questions that will help you and the group to grasp what he is saying.

- **Assertiveness and honesty**—the ability to be direct and open. The atmosphere of the group relies primarily, although not entirely, on the group facilitator. Your ability to be assertive and honest will help you to deal with problems that may arise, such as someone making a judgmental comment or giving negative advice. Facilitators need to be comfortable handling potential difficulties and awkward moments. Your assertiveness and honesty help provide a safe group environment.

- **An understanding of the purpose and needs of the group.** Most people who attend a group for the first time are uncomfortable and unsure of its purpose. Be ready to answer questions about the purpose of the group. In addition, it helps to be aware of the various needs of group members and how your group intends to deal with them.

- **Ability to be nonjudgmental**—an openness to different opinions and personalities. You help to establish a climate in which the group accepts different understandings of the causes of mental illness, and a variety of emotional responses to mental illness. If a member of the group holds beliefs which you oppose, you feel comfortable allowing him to speak his mind as long as he does not attempt to force his opinions on others.

- **Knowledge and experience with the Eight Stages.**

- **The ability to enjoy yourself**—to receive enjoyment from facilitating such groups. If leading the group is not something you want to do and will not enjoy—don't volunteer. It will not help the group to have a facilitator who would rather not lead.

- **Observation of the group's process**—the skill of assessing group behavior. This includes the ability to evaluate how well the group is handling certain issues. As facilitator, you should pay attention to whether participants encourage care taking or care giving behaviors. You can also assess this particular group's need during a given evening. For example, one night it may be beneficial to give more time to someone in crisis and allow the group to learn resourceful crisis intervention, while on another evening the group may need to be more playful.

- **Ability to give and receive suggestions and feedback.** Participants will want to express their thoughts about the group and sometimes about your facilitation techniques. Be open to their comments. To create a "comfort zone" within the group, leave some time at the end of each meeting to review it. Ask participants to tell the group what they liked best and least about the meeting. Ask how they think the group could improve.

Do not forget that as a self-help facilitator, you too are encouraged to take the time to receive support.

Now you have the basics for facilitating a self-help group. Remember that you are among peers who are willing to share the leadership and direction of the group. To make it simple, an outline of a typical group meeting is provided below:

A Sample Outline for Your Group

1. Start at a regular time and place. Greet each other.

2. Introduce yourself as the group facilitator for the evening and have the group sit in a circle.

3. Assure everyone that confidentiality is a requirement for participation and that names and personal information will not go beyond the group setting.

4. Ask someone to read the group's statement of purpose and/or the general guidelines.

5. Take time briefly to answer questions.

6. Ask everyone to Check-in. Use name tags (first names only) for groups of five or more.

7. Work on one of the Eight Stages. A technique which is effective is to have group members read through all the Eight Stage statements, working on a specific stage each evening.

8. Announce when and where the next meeting will be held and which stage will be discussed.

9. Take time for closing statements where participants can respond to the meeting, and give feedback. During closing statements it is important to let the group members express themselves without interruptions from others.

Building Friendships

In many groups, each participant gets together with another participant outside the regular meetings. This time can be used to get to know one another better, or discuss the stage the group is working on that week. You may want to pick someone in your group to get together with between group meetings. A great technique to encourage cohesiveness and build friendships is to have the group commit to calling one group member a week. During the week's check-in, members can acknowledge whom they called.

EXCHANGING ADVICE

Many people attend a self-help group not only for support but also to receive advice on dealing with their dilemmas. In general, however, it is wise to be very cautious about offering your opinions or allowing others to give theirs, *unless advice is solicited*. Make certain that the person speaking wants advice; he may need only to share his experiences. In general, if someone wants advice it is up to him to ask for it. When you feel a strong urge to help someone by giving him recommendations, first ask him if he is interested in hearing your ideas. If he says no, respect his wishes.

When advice or ideas are solicited, offer them in a nonjudgmental tone. Share your personal experience dealing with a similar challenge, describing the obstacles you encountered. Remember, your idea is only one of many possible ways to solve a problem. Offer your opinion as you would a gift, allowing the listener to do with it as he chooses. In fact, the group members may benefit more from learning how to generate their own alternatives through the process of imaginative problem-solving described in Chapter 6. This encourages the person seeking advice to come up with some alternatives on his own.

In addition to working on the Eight Stages, some groups choose to discuss other themes relevant to families of the mentally ill. Suggested themes for groups include the following:

- Caretaking versus caregiving—In what way and to what extent are family members responsible for the present and future of their mentally ill relative?
- Children—What are the concerns in deciding whether or not to have children?
- Identity—How does a close relative's mental illness affect his perception of himself and others?
- Crisis—How can families deal effectively with a crisis?
- Relationships—How does the relative's mental illness affect his relationships with friends, spouse, parents, or employer/employees ?
- Resources—What resources are available in the community for families of the mentally ill, and what is the easiest way to gain access to them?

Here is an opportunity for your group to address these issues with each other's help. Remember, however, that there are no right or wrong answers to these difficult questions.

Self-help groups are like families. When you are involved with a self-help group, observe how you react and feel in the group. If you have a tendency to be a Caretaker in your family you are likely to react as a Caretaker in your group. If you have felt victimized by your family, you may begin to feel victimized by the members of your self-help group. That's good, because it gives you a wonderful opportunity to change the self-defeating habits you engage in and replace them with positive, life-enhancing behaviors. The self-help group offers you an opportunity to practice being a Caregiver—someone who can be involved with others but not overwhelmed by their problems.

Parting Words

You are a precious resource. If you do not feel this about

yourself, you need help from others to realize this is the truth about you. When you set down this book, take a brief rest, then get out that note book and begin your journal and work on the Eight Stages. Unseal that spring of love and creativity inside of you. Reach out for help. Begin now.

To order tapes, books, the Training Manual for Facilitators, or to receive information regarding the training seminars and workshops on the Eight Stage Healing Process write or call:

The Eight Stages
P.O. Box 24598
Edina, Minnesota 55424

(612) 872-1565

ABOUT THE AUTHOR

Julie Tallard Johnson is a psychotherapist who has pioneered healing resources for siblings and adult children of the mentally ill. She is founder of the Siblings and Adult Children's Network, a committee of the National Alliance for the Mentally Ill. She is author of several self-help books for young adults. She speaks to groups around the country about issues such as self-esteem, healthy relationships, and mindfulness meditation. She conducts Eight Stage training seminars. She lives in Minneapolis, Minnesota where she has an active practice. She has a brother who struggles with schizophrenia.

Also by Julie Tallard Johnson

Understanding Mental Illness: A Book for Teens Who Care About Someone With Mental Illness., 1989, Lerner Publications

Celebrate You: Building Your Self-esteem., 1990, Lerner Publications

Making Friends Finding Love: A Book About Teen Relationships., 1992, Lerner Publications

The Eight Stage Healing Process: A Manual for Facilitators., 1989, 1994, PEMA Publications

Facilitators of Self-Esteem: A Guide for Teachers and Group Leaders., 1993, PEMA Publications